# THE TOTALLY BRILLIANT
# PUZZLE
# AND DRAWING BOOK

 ARCTURUS

ARCTURUS

This edition published in 2012 by Arcturus Publishing Limited
26/27 Bickels Yard, 151–153 Bermondsey Street,
London SE1 3HA

Copyright © 2012 Arcturus Publishing Limited

All rights reserved. No part of this publication may be reproduced,
stored in a retrieval system, or transmitted, in any form or by any means,
electronic, mechanical, photocopying, recording or otherwise, without
prior written permission in accordance with the provisions of the
Copyright Act 1956 (as amended). Any person or persons who do any
unauthorised act in relation to this publication may be liable to criminal
prosecution and civil claims for damages.

ISBN: 978-1-84858-472-3
CH002162EN
Supplier 16, Date 0812, Print Run 1771

Printed in Singapore

# GOING APE

Take a careful look at the picture to see if you
can spot all of the items from the list.

Find these items!

# MISSING MONSTER

One of the monsters from the top picture is missing in the bottom picture. Can you spot which one it is?

# PIRATE PAIRS

All of these pirates have an identical twin - except one. Can you find him?

# THE SECRET GARDEN

What would you love to see if you found a secret garden?

# ALL MIXED UP

Match the boxes in pairs to make the names of ten different plants, trees and flowers. One has been done to help you.

TUS
TLE
GUS
BAM
LET
WIL
BON
NET
SAI
CRO
ORC
LOW
BOO
CAC
HID
CUS
FUN
VER
CLO
VIO

| C | A | C | T | U | S |
|---|---|---|---|---|---|

# GOTCHA!

What has this monster spider caught in its giant web?

# JURASSIC JOKE

Use this decoder to work out the answer to the dino-joke.

| A | B | C | D | E | F | G | H | I | J | K | L | M | N | O | P | Q | R | S | T | U | V | W | X | Y | Z |
|---|---|---|---|---|---|---|---|---|---|---|---|---|---|---|---|---|---|---|---|---|---|---|---|---|---|
| Z | Y | X | W | V | U | T | S | R | Q | P | O | N | M | L | K | J | I | H | G | F | E | D | C | B | A |

**What do you call a dinosaur that smashes everything in its path?**

## GBIZMMLHZFIFH DIVXPH!

_ _ _ _ _ _ _ _ _ _ _ _ _ _ _ _ _ _ !

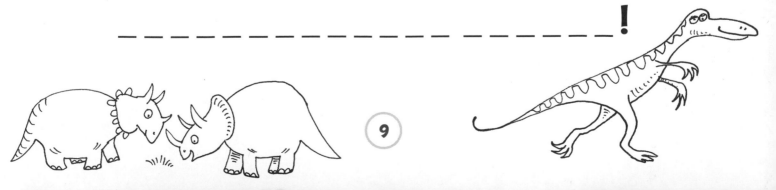

# EGGS-ACTLY

Some of the letters of the alphabet are missing from these eggs. Work out which they are and then use them to spell the name of a bird.

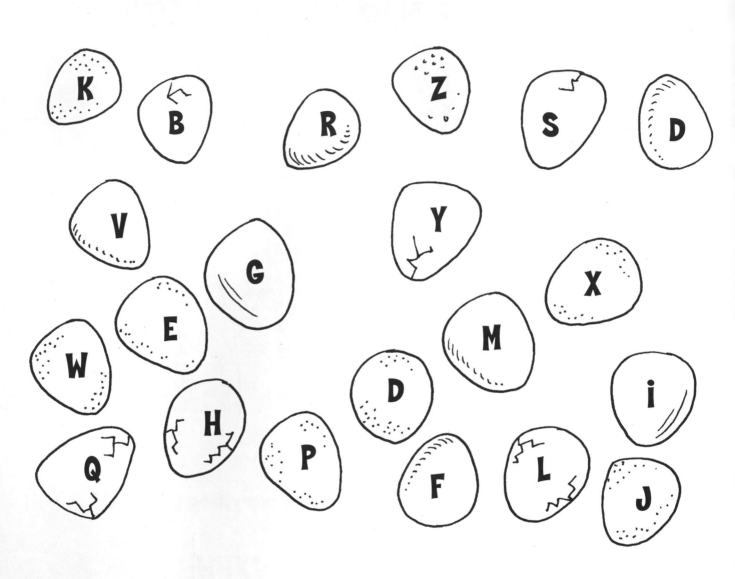

The missing letters are: _ _ _ _ _ _ _

The bird is: _ _ _ _ _ _ _

# WEIRD SEARCH

Find ten weird or creepy creatures hidden in the grid. There are no clues to help you!

```
Z L V A M P I R E G
W L W I Z L G F G Z
O I O A G L L H N O
E E Z G H O U L A M
W W Z A W R W G I B
O G W E R T I W T I
L G R I E D Z E R E
L E R Y T E V R A R
W E E E W C A E M A
W G H T S O H G E W
```

# POLLEN COUNT

How many smaller flowers make up the four big flowers?

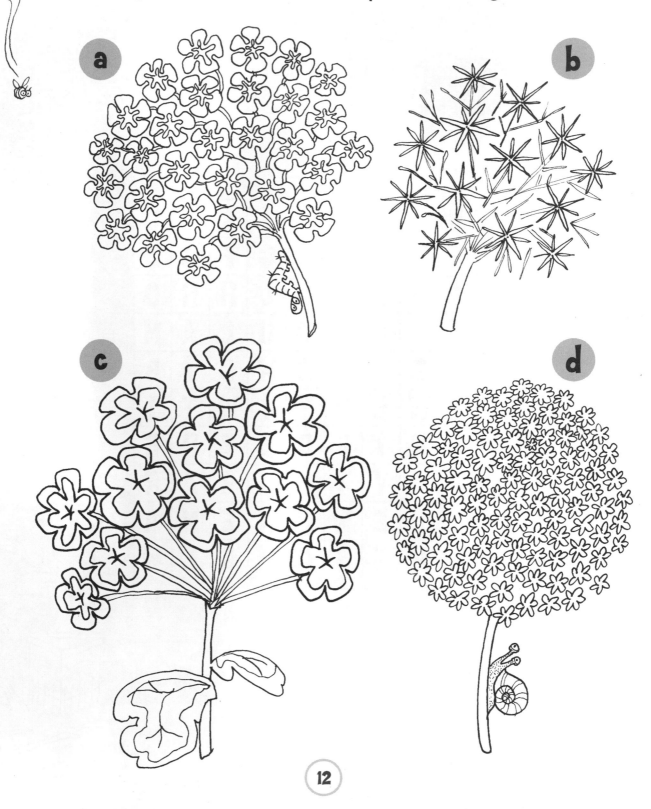

# BIRDS GALORE

Fill this scene with as many different birds as you can think of.

# OUT OF THIS WORLD!

Only one of these alien actors can make it in the movies.
Which of them is going to star in the next blockbuster?

1. It has more than two eyes.
2. It has two legs.
3. It has only one head.
4. It isn't wearing any clothes.

# HELP!

This dinosaur needs some protection. Can you draw on some spikes and scales?

# SEEING STRIPES

Which of these zebras is the odd one out?

# THE NAME GAME

On each line, find the letter that appears in every name.
Use these letters to spell the name of the old pirate!

| GIO | EGBERT | CRAIG | OGDEN | _ |
| BJORN | OWEN | CODY | JOHN | _ |
| NATHAN | DANTE | NOEL | ANDREW | _ |
| FAIZ | ZAINAB | EZRA | OZZY | _ |
| CALEB | DALE | BLAKE | AARON | _ |
| ALI | BAILEY | LAWSON | RIDLEY | _ |
| TONY | NOAH | OLAF | DIEGO | _ |

# BUTTERFLY BONANZA

Which of the butterflies has numbers on its wings that add up to exactly 100?

# POND DIPPING

What amazing creatures have you found in the water?

# PIRATE PEDRO

Draw the pirate that belongs to this parrot!

# TRICERATOPS TRAIL

Work out the sums on each Triceratops and find a path to the jungle by hopping on dinosaurs with 3 as the answer.

START

17 – 14

$^1/_3$ x 3

14 – 7

36 ÷ 12

9 ÷ 2

33 ÷ 3

3 x 2

1·5 x 2

99 – 96

13 – 3

7 x 0·5

14 ÷ 7

6 ÷ 2

FINISH

10 – 7

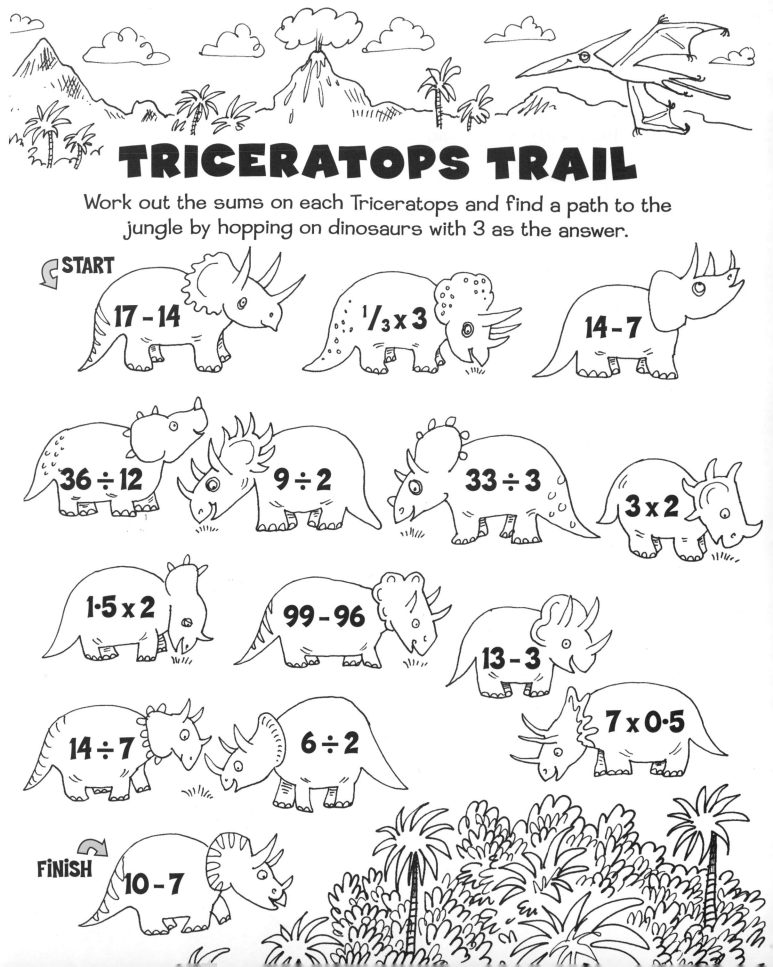

# PIG OUT!

This greedy pig has had too much to eat, as usual! Fill his belly with everything he has stuffed his snout with.

# IN A MUDDLE

Help Pirates Stoppit and Shuttup untangle the ropes to spell out the name of the island they are sailing to.

| D | U | M | R | E | B | A |
|---|---|---|---|---|---|---|

# PRINCESS PETS

Draw a selection of cute or exotic pets for Princess Padmani.

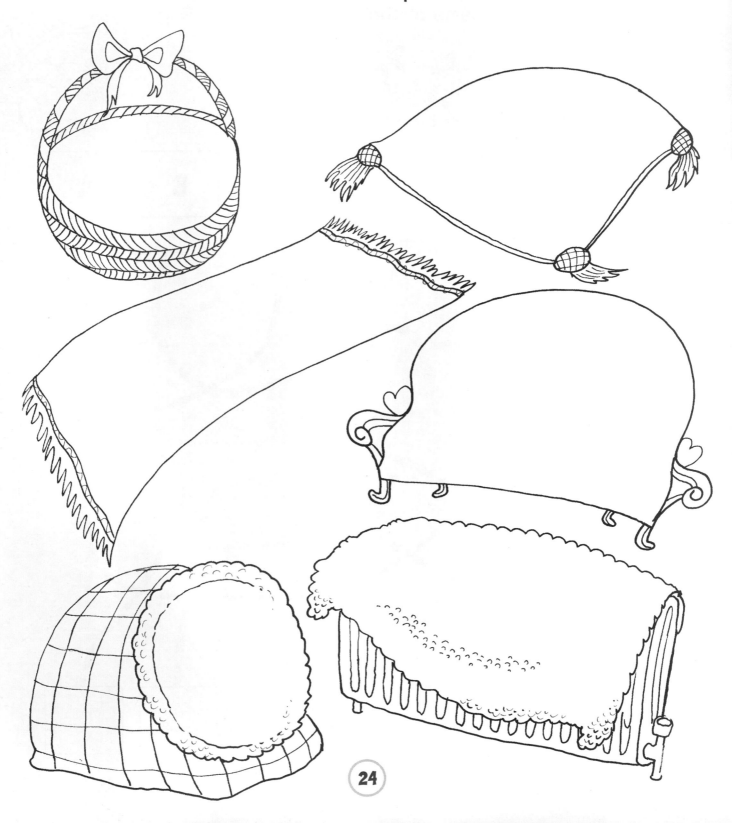

# BIG IS BEAUTIFUL

Work out each sum to find which of the giant
water lilies has the biggest number.

(2 x 10) + 13 =

(56 – 41) + 17 =

1000 ÷ 50 =

7 x 3 x 2 =

105 ÷ 3 =

# TAKING A NAP

Who is snoozing in the coffin?

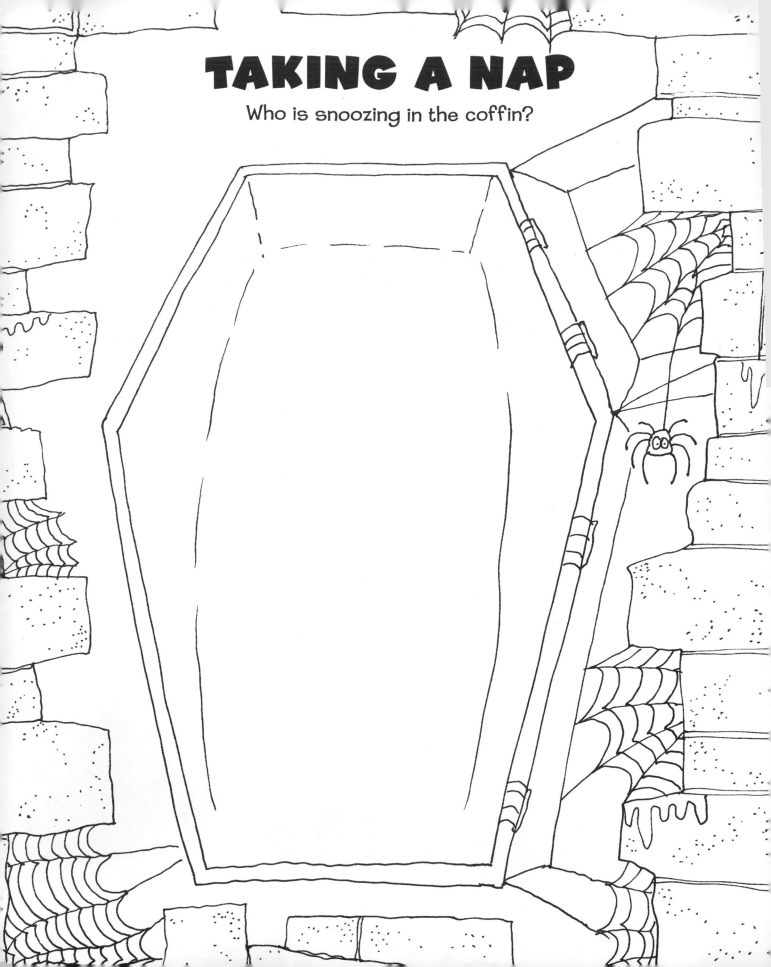

# MUNCH TIME

Which of the jigsaw pieces finishes the puzzle?

a    b    c    d    e

# THE RIGHT FIT

Write the listed creatures in the correct place in the grid,
and the circled letters will spell another animal.

**AARDVARK**
**BULLFROG**

**CHIPMUNK**
**ELEPHANT**

**FLAMINGO**
**HORNBILL**

**MONGOOSE**
**PARAKEET**

# EYE SPY

What do you think Pirate Pedro can see through his telescope?

# FAIRY FOOD

Which of the toadstools is safe for Fairy Freya to pick?

It doesn't have spots.
It hasn't got a dark stripe
around the edge.
It hasn't got a pointed top.
It has a thin stalk.

# HONEY TRAP

How many of the bees are heading back to the hive?

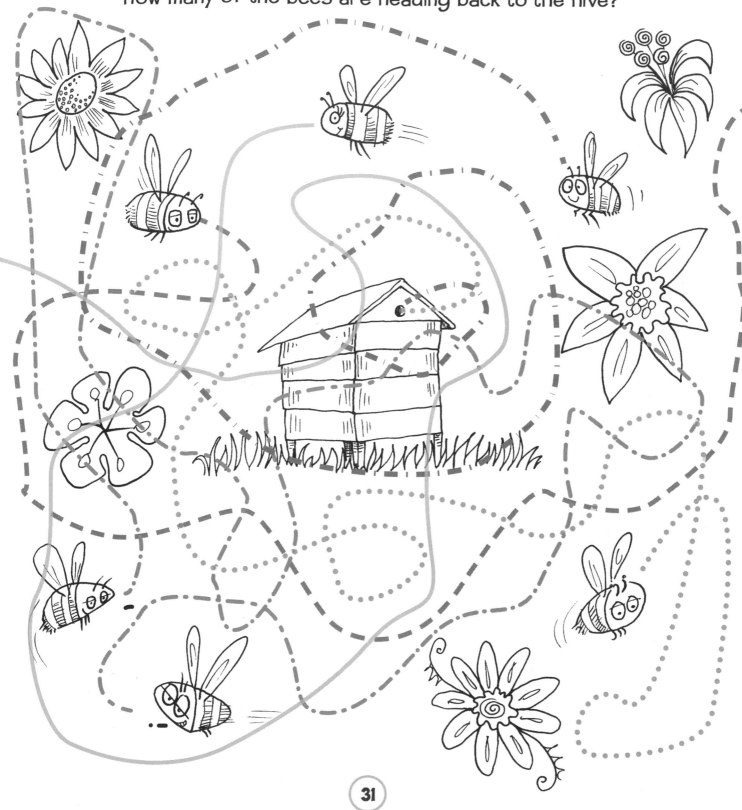

# ON REFLECTION

A vampire has no reflection... but can you read what the mirror message says?

What do vampire movie stars often receive?

Fang mail!

# DINO DESIGN

Draw some friendly dinosaurs on to these clothes.

# FEEDING TIME

Write down the letters shown by the minute hand, then the hour hand, for each listed time. They will spell the names of the animals being fed.

__ __ / __ __    Quarter to two.

__ __ / __ __    Twenty past eight.

__ __ / __ __    Half past eleven.

__ __ / __ __    3 o'clock.

__ __ / __ __    Twenty five past ten.

__ __ / __ __    Twenty five to one.

# MANY MAGGOTS

Fill in the answers to the sums on the pirates' maggoty bread.

40 + 63 =

72 − 53 =

81 ÷ 9 =

5 x 6 =

27 + 27 =

86 − 39 =

7 x 3 =

48 ÷ 6 =

# IVORY TOWER

Which of the strands of ivy leads all the way to Princess Isadora?

a    b    c    d    e

# A BIRD'S EYE VIEW

Look at the main picture of the botanical gardens and then work out which of the smaller pictures is how it would look to a bird flying overhead.

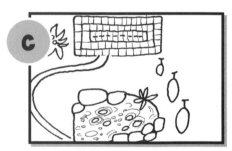

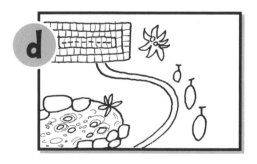

# ANIMAL ALERT!

Watch out, there's a wild animal about! Design a road sign to warn drivers that something unusual may be crossing ahead...

# DINO DIGITS

Pair up these Megalosaurus by working out each sum and matching two dinosaurs that have the same answer.

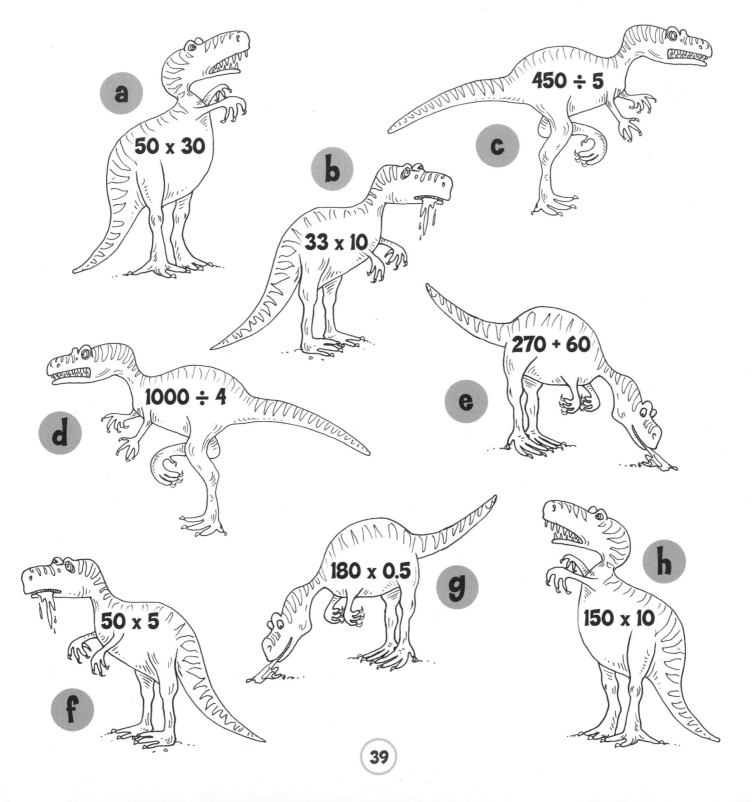

a  50 x 30

b  33 x 10

c  450 ÷ 5

d  1000 ÷ 4

e  270 + 60

f  50 x 5

g  180 x 0.5

h  150 x 10

# MONSTER MATCH

Only two of these monsters are identical. Can you see which two?

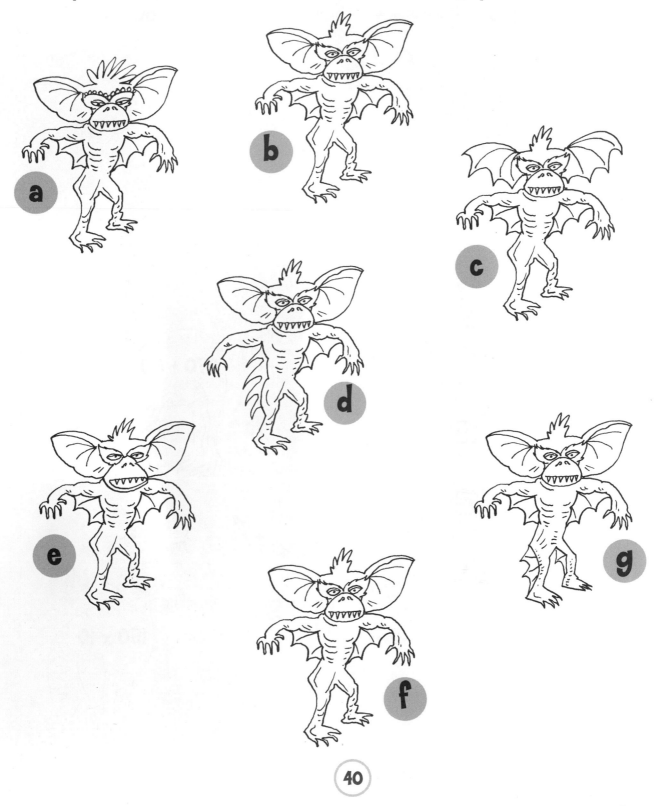

# LAND AHOY!

The pirate ship has sighted land. Can you spot ten differences between the two pictures?

# DANDELION CLOCK

Use the letters on the seeds with
four wings to spell out what time it is.

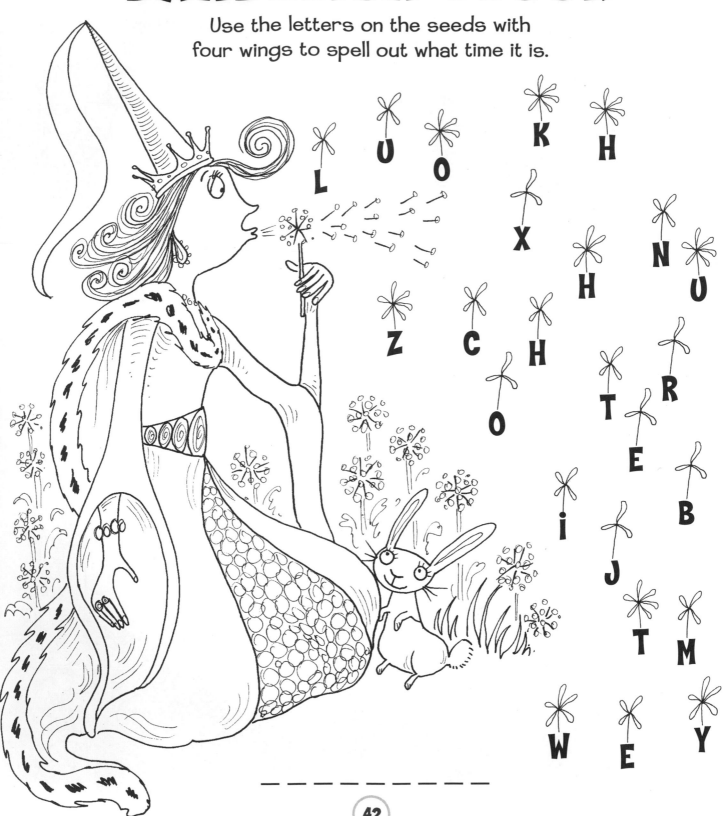

L   U   O   K   H

X   H   N   U

Z   C   H

O   T   R

i   E   B

J

T   M

W   E   Y

\_ \_ \_ \_ \_ \_ \_ \_ \_ \_

# A-MAZING

Work your way through the rings on the tree trunk to get to the middle.

# SCAREDY CAT

What has frightened this cat?

# DINOSAURS AND DRAGONS

How many dragonflies can you count in this scene?

# PAIR UP THE PETS

Use the clues to put ticks and crosses in the grid to work out which person has each pet, and what kind of fur it has.

1. Freddie's pet doesn't meow.
2. Luke has a black pet.
3. Freddie's pet isn't brown or a dog.
4. The boys have the cat and the hamster.

|         | dog | cat | hamster | white | brown | black |
|---------|-----|-----|---------|-------|-------|-------|
| Annika  |     |     |         |       |       |       |
| Luke    |     |     |         |       |       |       |
| Freddie |     |     |         |       |       |       |

# JUNGLE ISLAND

Imagine you have landed on a faraway island.
What - or who - is hiding in the jungle?

# SHOE SHUFFLE

Princess Pedora is tidying her room. Can you find three shoes that aren't in pairs?

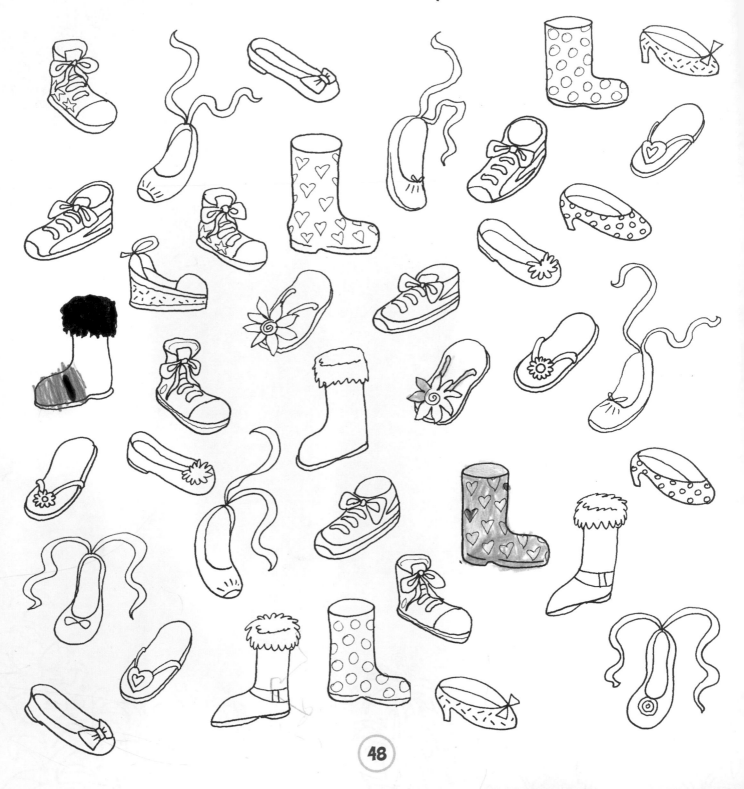

# GOING UNDERGROUND

Follow each path and choose the correct trails to spell the names of three burrowing mammals.

# SPELL SHOP

Can you work out how much it will cost to make up this invisibility spell?

Sale

Nightfall — **7** Gold Coins

Sloth Moss — **6** Gold Coins per kilo

DOG SNORES — **3** Gold Coins

Bat's Wings **0.5** Gold Coin each

Cats Eyes **1** Gold Coin each

Elder Root **1** Gold Coin per kilo

Spider's Web **2** Gold Coins per m

**5** Gold Coins Moon Dust

## Invisibility Spell

2x bat's wings
4x cat's eyes
1.5 m spider's web
1 jar of nightfall

Invisibility spell =
_ _ coins

# MIGHTY MIX UP

What would a T. rex and a Brachiosaurus
look like if they got mixed up?

# THINK ABOUT IT...

Use the code to work out the answer to the joke.

What shape is a parrot that has flown away?

The answer is: _ _ _ _ _ _ _ _

| | |
|---|---|
| A | ✺ |
| B | ◉ |
| C | ✳ |
| D | ❄ |
| E | ✻ |
| F | ✳ |
| G | ✳ |
| H | ✳ |
| I | ✳ |
| J | ✳ |
| K | ✳ |
| L | ● |
| M | ○ |
| N | ■ |
| O | ◻ |
| P | ◻ |
| Q | ◻ |
| R | ◻ |
| S | ▲ |
| T | ▼ |
| U | ◆ |
| V | ❖ |
| W | ◗ |
| X | ✳ |
| Y | ✳ |
| Z | ✳ |

# MINI BEASTS

Which mini beast finishes the sequence here: a spider, snail or beetle?

# DRESS DESIGNER

Add the details to make this ball gown extra special.

# PRETTY POLLY

Reunite Pirate Melville with his parrot, Moby, by counting in threes, starting at the number 3.

START

| 54 | 51 | 48 | 45 | 12 | 9 | 6 | 3 |
| 57 | 66 | 69 | 42 | 15 | 18 | 21 | 26 |
| 60 | 63 | 72 | 39 | 36 | 27 | 24 | 32 |
| | | 75 | 78 | 33 | 30 | | |
| | | 85 | 81 | 35 | | | |
| | | | 84 | 87 | | | |
| 102 | 99 | 96 | 93 | 90 | 94 | | |

FINISH

# FORTUNE TELLING

Cross out every other letter, starting with the letter that's blackest,
to find the names of two scary characters you don't want to meet.

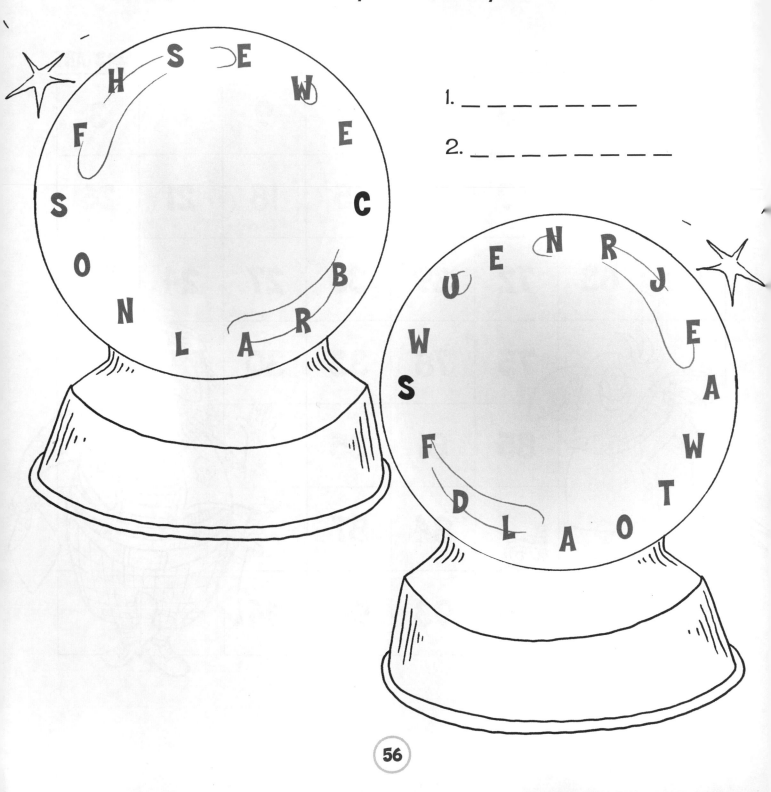

1. _ _ _ _ _ _ _

2. _ _ _ _ _ _ _ _

# TOO TROO

Which of the small pictures of Troodon matches the main picture?

# CAGE CODE

Solve the sums and cross out each answer in the grid. You should have four remaining numbers to unlock the tiger's cage door.

71 x 2 =

1000 ÷ 100 =

900 – 6 =

25 x 100 =

2468 ÷ 2 =

999 ÷ 3 =

416 x 2 =

11 x 11 =

7 x 30 =

60 ÷ 5 =

| 1 | 1 | 8 | 3 | 2 | 8 |
|---|---|---|---|---|---|
| 0 | 2 | 6 | 2 | 1 | 9 |
| 3 | 3 | 3 | 5 | 2 | 4 |
| 1 | 4 | 2 | 0 | 1 | 2 |
| 9 | 2 | 1 | 0 | 2 | 4 |

Enter code here

# SEADOG SUDOKU

Fill in the puzzle so that every row, column and mini-grid has each of the six pirate pictures.

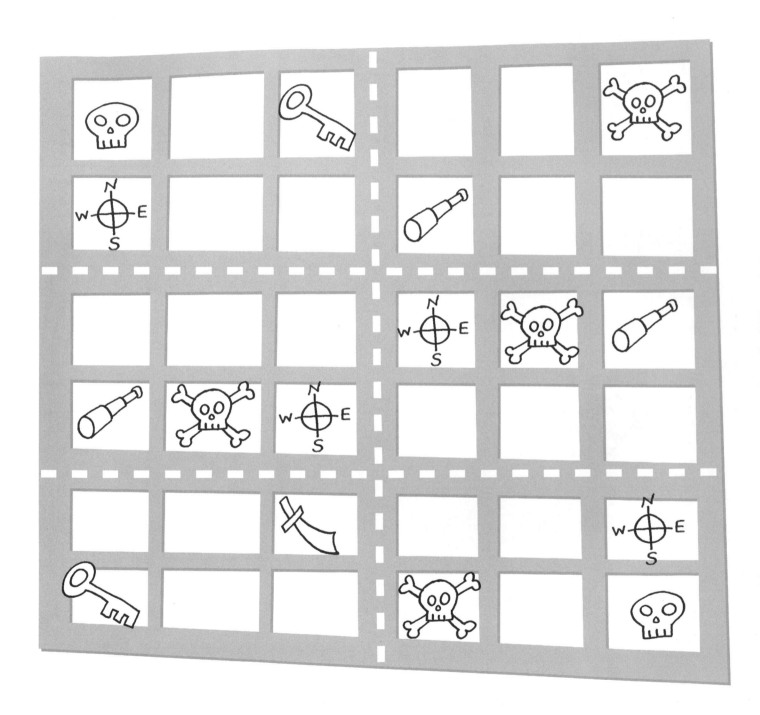

# RING RING

What completes the pattern here?

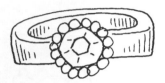  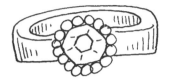

 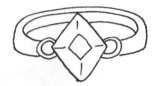 

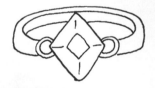 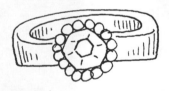 **?**

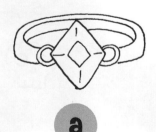 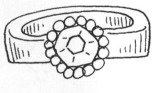 

a b c

# HATCHING OUT

What creatures are coming out of these eggs?

# BEASTLY BEING

Which of the groups of words cannot be rearranged to spell GARGOYLE correctly?

GGOLYARE

LAYGOREG

GREGOYAL

GOGLEYOR

GLOGARYE

REALGOGY

YEARGLOG

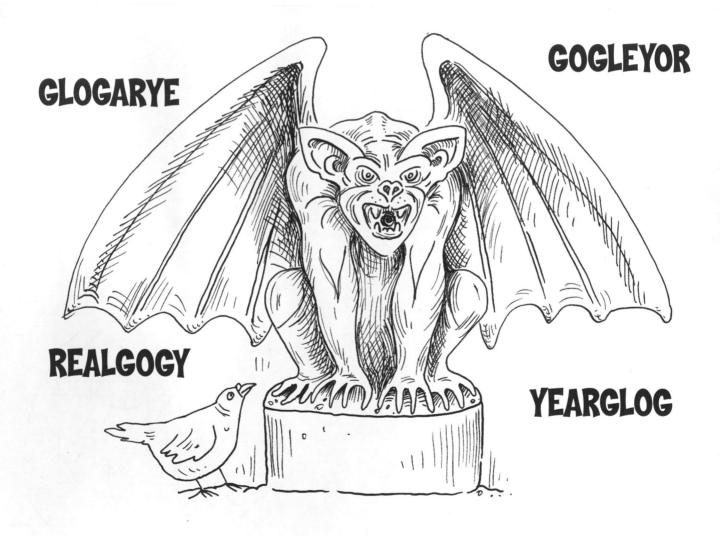

# DINOSAUR WORLD

Answer the questions using the map and grid references.

1. In which square do you climb up the Dino Slide?
2. Where can you eat your picnic, E3 or E5?
3. What can you buy in B2?
4. Which dinosaur welcomes you on a walk at B4?

# ON SAFARI

What amazing African creatures have you spotted through your binoculars?

# BARREL OF FUN

How many times can you find the
word AHOY hidden in the grid?

| | | | | | | | | | | | |
|---|---|---|---|---|---|---|---|---|---|---|---|
| A | A | Y | Y | H | A | O | A | Y | H | O | Y |
| A | H | A | O | A | A | H | H | O | O | H | A |
| O | H | A | H | O | H | A | O | A | Y | A | Y |
| A | H | Y | H | O | H | O | H | O | O | Y | O |
| A | H | A | O | O | Y | Y | O | Y | H | H | H |
| H | Y | H | Y | A | O | Y | H | H | A | A | H |
| Y | A | O | A | H | Y | Y | A | Y | O | O | O |
| A | H | Y | H | A | H | O | Y | A | O | H | A |
| Y | O | O | H | A | H | A | H | O | A | Y | H |
| A | H | A | A | H | O | Y | A | O | O | H | A |
| H | O | Y | H | O | A | H | O | O | A | O | H |
| O | H | H | Y | H | O | Y | O | H | O | Y | O |
| A | O | H | O | Y | A | H | Y | O | H | A | H |
| A | H | A | H | A | Y | O | H | O | Y | O | O |

# RIGHT ROYAL WRONGS

Can you spot six things that are wrong in this picture?

# TREE TIMES TABLE

Work out the answers to the sums using the number code.
Write the answers as numbers.

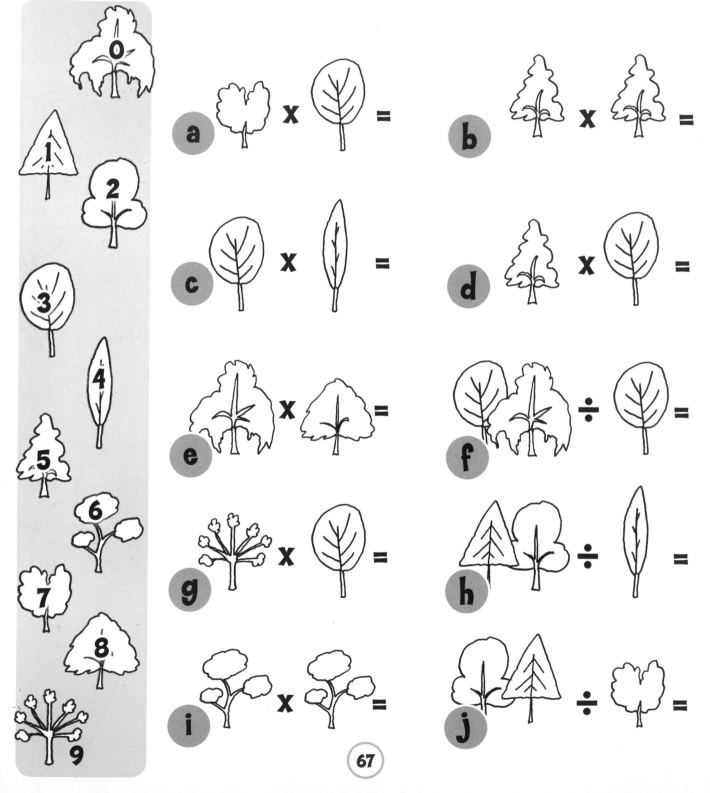

# ALIENS HAVE LANDED

Aliens have landed from another planet! Draw them here.

# TIME OUT

Write down the letters shown by the minute hand, then the hour hand, for each listed time. They will spell out the names of two dinosaurs.

**a** quarter past eight, half past ten, twenty past twelve

_ _ _ _ _ _ _ _ _ _ _

**b** five to seven, ten past nine, twenty five past one

_ _ _ _ _ _ _ _ _ _ _

# CREATURE CARVINGS

How many creatures are carved on this tree trunk?

# T-SHIRT TREASURES

Add logos, patterns and lots of embellishments to these T-shirts.
Which one do you like best?

# WISH ME LUCK

How many lucky horseshoes can you count in the royal stables?

# BEETLE MANIA

Which of these stag beetle silhouettes matches the main picture?

# MONSTER LAUGHS

Cross out the words using the instructions below. The words left will be the answer to the joke.

## Why did the monster eat a lamp?

1. Any word with more than 7 letters.
2. Words that begin with T.
3. Words containing the letter O.

| NO | SOME | ONE | THE |
|----|------|-----|-----|
| SO | BECAUSE | HE | WOULD |
| COULD | WANTED | TORCH | A |
| TOOK | TEACHERS | LIGHT | LOOK |
| SNACK | MOON | SWALLOW | BEDROOMS |

# NEW DISCOVERIES

Draw what you think these crazy dinosaurs would look like.

**ALLIGATOSAURUS**

**SPIKODON**

**SHOOTORAPTOR**

**STRIPEOSAURUS**

# NEW FACES

There are three new animals in the bottom picture. Can you spot them all?

# PIRATE LOGIC

Read the clues carefully and work out which Captain owns each ship, what size parrot he has, and what his parrot is called.

**1.** Captain Barnacle is the captain of the first ship.
**2.** The parrot called Pesky lives on ship 2.
**3.** Captain Scablegs has a parrot called Potty.
**4.** The biggest parrot is called Perky.
**5.** Captain Greybeard's parrot isn't the small one.
**6.** One of the parrots is medium sized.

|  | Ship 1 | Ship 2 | Ship 3 |
|---|---|---|---|
| Pirate |  |  |  |
| Parrot |  |  |  |
| Size |  |  |  |

# DESIGN A DINOSAUR

Doodle your own dinosaur by joining up these bones.

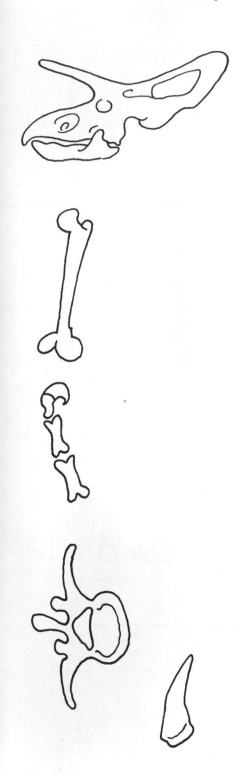

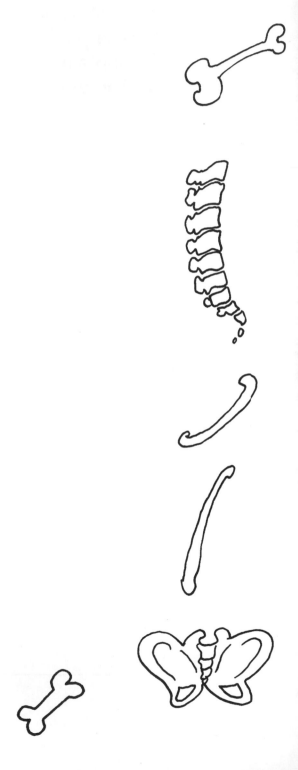

78

# NATURE HUNT

Find the names of ten trees hidden in the wordsearch grid.
There is no list to help you!

| W | A | R | U | T | W | i | L | L | O | W |
|---|---|---|---|---|---|---|---|---|---|---|
| S | B | E | E | C | H | U | E | T | L | G |
| Y | O | R | S | B | B | A | Q | E | N | R |
| C | A | X | A | P | F | Q | M | P | H | V |
| A | V | R | C | N | J | T | i | S | Z | P |
| M | K | G | A | W | C | L | W | O | F | O |
| O | A | K | T | B | C | H | M | i | T | P |
| R | S | Y | L | R | X | K | C | Y | G | L |
| E | M | R | D | Y | U | F | D | L | K | A |
| Z | C | H | E | S | T | N | U | T | N | R |
| G | L | E | K | P | N | G | K | E | X | M |
| B | A | S | H | R | Z | i | W | H | U | F |
| J | H | A | F | U | O | P | i | N | E | L |
| E | U | D | B | C | i | S | C | J | D | Q |
| A | P | P | L | E | T | P | C | V | K | E |

There are also five tree-related words hidden diagonally.
Can you find those, too?

# CHAIN REACTION

Which of the jigsaw pieces finishes the puzzle?

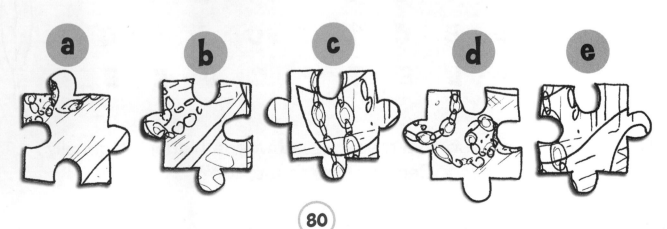

a     b     c     d     e

# FOSSIL FINDER

If A=1, B=2, C=3 and so on, can you label the boxes of bones correctly?

# MONKEY PUZZLE

Use the letter pairs on the coconuts to help the monkey spell
the names of three of the largest animals in the world.

EL
OC
ER
OS
HI
OP
EP
NT
PP
AM
HA
iN
US
OT
RH

\_ \_ \_ \_ \_ \_ \_ \_ \_ \_ NT

\_ \_ PP \_ \_ \_ \_ \_ \_ \_ \_

\_ \_ \_ \_ OC \_ \_ \_ \_ \_

# FINDING YOUR WAY

Find the correct path from start to finish,
following the pictures in this order:

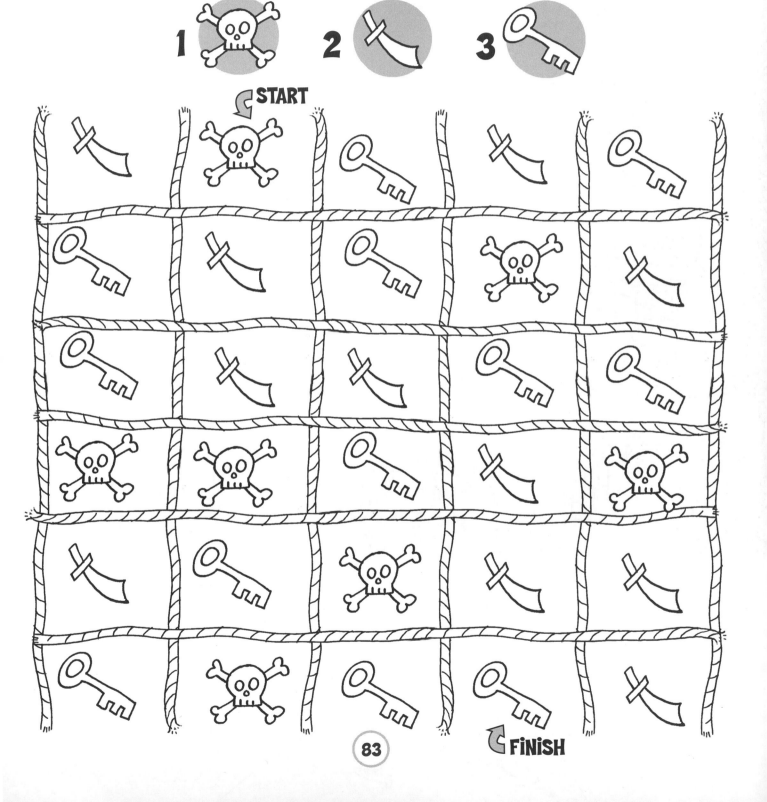

83

# TOWER TABLES

Which of the palace towers does NOT have a
number from the 6 times table?

# UNDER COVER

Draw a background for each creature, and then add some patterns on the bodies to keep them camouflaged.

# MEET THE MISFITS!

Study the sequence of pictures correctly and work out which of these creepy females finishes the pattern: a, b or c?

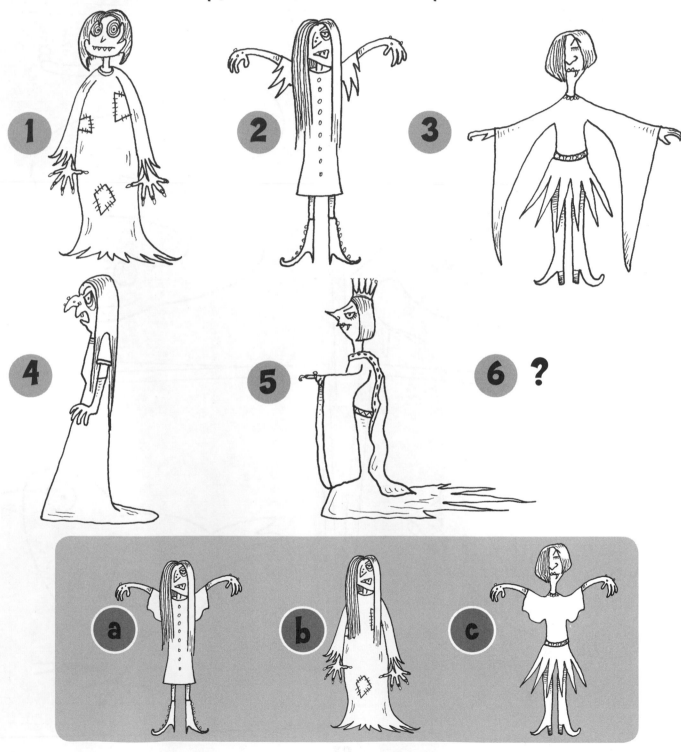

# DINO DAZE

Find a path from row A to row F by following the tails of the dinosaurs. If it points down, you move down, or if it points sideways, follow it sideways.

START

|   |   |   |   |   |   |
|---|---|---|---|---|---|
| **A** | | | | | |
| **B** | | | | | |
| **C** | | | | | |
| **D** | | | | | |
| **E** | | | | | |
| **F** | | | | | |

FINISH

# BRANCHING OUT

What creature is hanging around in the trees?

# SAFE PORT

Batten down the hatches! Follow the directions across the stormy seas and draw an X in the port where the pirates should land.

**1.** Sail east for two squares.
**2.** Head north three squares.
**3.** Follow your course east for two more squares.
**4.** Head south and cast your anchor in safe waters.

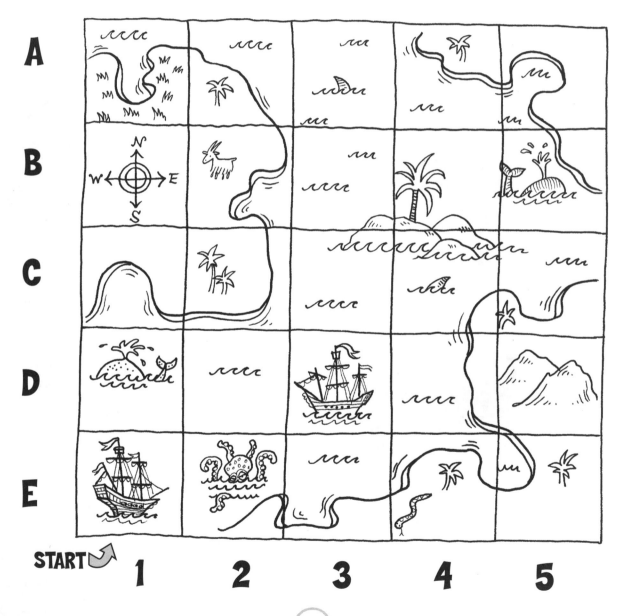

# CROWNING GLORY

Cross out any letter that appears more than once
to find where Princess Annalise lives.

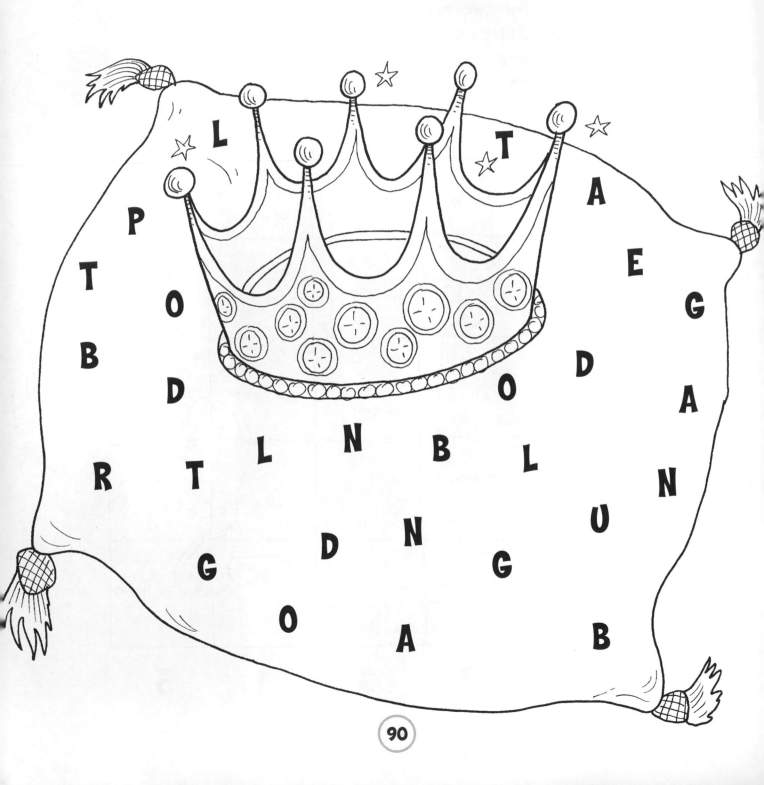

# THROUGH THE LOOKING GLASS

Which is the only one of the magnified images that could be part of the main picture?

# TRICK OR TREAT?

Draw scary faces on these Hallowe'en masks to freak out your friends!

# DINO-DOKU

Fill in the puzzle so that every row, column and mini-grid has each of the six dino pictures.

# CAT CONUNDRUM

Which of the groups of words cannot be rearranged to correctly spell a big cat?

ARGUJA  THERMAP

GRITE  REPNTAH

HETHACE  OGURAC

DRAPOLE

# WANTED!

Design a poster to catch the
world's most wanted pirate.

**Pirate** _____

**Distinguishing features** _____

_____

_____

**Last seen** _____

**Reward** _____

# MIRROR MIRROR

Can you read the answer to the joke in
Princess Hannah's mirror?

**Where did the ice queen go to dance?**

The snow ball!

# AS THE CROW FLIES

Which of the crows has flown the farthest from the nests? Add up the numbers to find out.

# SPOOKY SPELLINGS

How many smaller words can you make from the letters below?

## THE WITCHING HOUR

1 WITH

2 THING

3 _____

4 _____

5 _____

6 _____

7 _____

8 _____

9 _____

10 _____

11 _____

12 _____

# FLYING HIGH

What would flying reptiles look like if you were in charge?
Add feathers, claws, teeth and patterns.

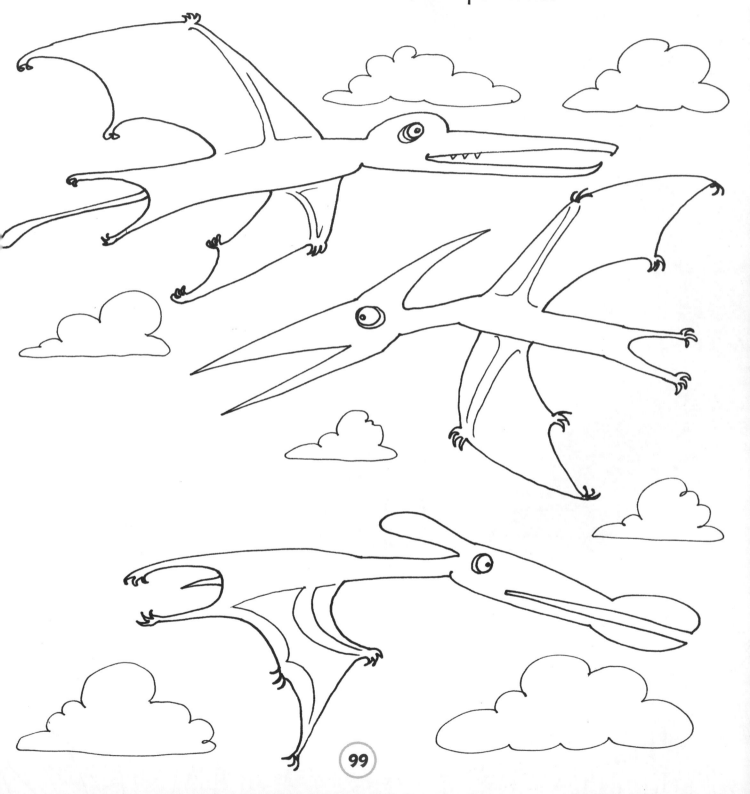

# REALLY RARE

Find the word PANDA hidden only once in the grid.

| P | A | N | N | A | P | N | A |
|---|---|---|---|---|---|---|---|
| N | P | D | N | A | A | A | P |
| D | A | N | P | D | N | D | A |
| A | D | A | A | P | D | N | N |
| P | A | P | A | N | D | A | A |
| P | A | N | N | A | D | N | P |
| A | A | D | D | P | D | A | N |
| A | N | D | A | A | D | D | N |
| A | P | A | D | D | P | A | N |
| N | A | D | A | N | A | D | P |
| D | N | A | P | A | N | N | A |
| A | A | P | N | N | D | A | D |
| D | P | A | D | N | D | D | N |
| N | A | N | N | P | A | N | A |
| A | N | D | P | A | D | N | A |

# RUFUS REDBEARD

Use the clues to work out which of the flags belongs to Rufus Redbeard.

1. It has a single skull on it.
2. It doesn't show any weapons.
3. The skull is facing forwards.
4. It only shows two bones.

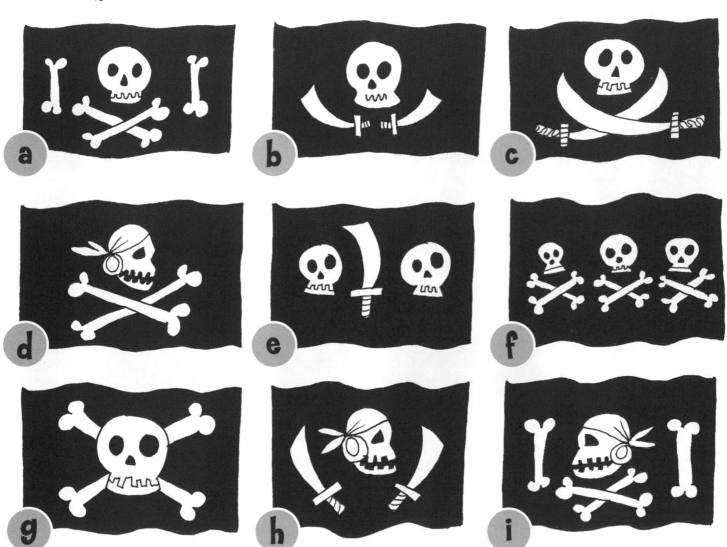

# PRINCESS SUDOKU

Fill in the puzzle so that every row, column and mini-grid has each of the six pictures.

# UGLY BUG BALL

Which three bugs have made their way into the
ugly bug ball in the bottom picture?

# WHO GOES THERE?

What are the people running away from? Tilt the page towards you to read the answer.

# THUMBS UP

This Iguanodon likes to spell things properly! Tick five dinosaur names that are correct.

- ☐ BRACHIASAURUS
- ☐ TRISERATOPS
- ☐ VELOCIRAPTOR
- ☐ ALLASAURUS
- ☐ GIGANTOSAURUS
- ☐ STEGGOSAURUS
- ☐ PTERANODON
- ☐ TYRANNOSAURUS
- ☐ SPINOSAURUS

# EAGLE EYES

Follow the tangled lines to see which
eagle belongs in each nest.

# DEADLY DICE

Do the sums shown on the skull dice to see which roll is the highest.
Each time, do the adding part of the sum and then the multiplication.

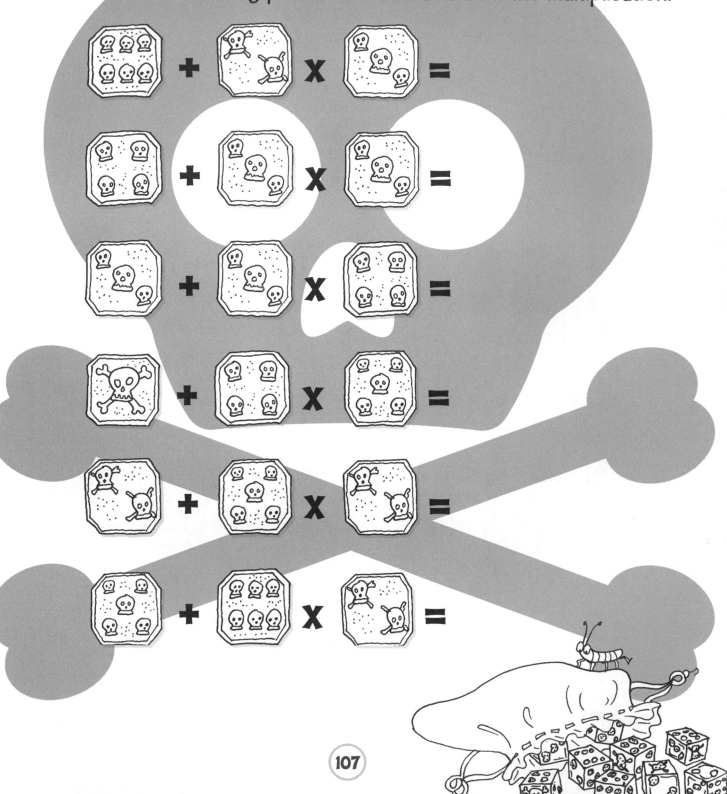

# FASHION BY YOU

Finish off these clothes with decorations, and then add accessories to match.

# MAKING TRACKS

Why do bears have fur coats? Work out the
answer using the picture code.

# SCARY MOVIE

Finish the poster for a horror movie. What will be the scary star?

COMING SOON!

Starring

# ON THEIR TRAIL

Starting at J, find all of the listed dinosaur words in one long, continuous trail through the grid. They're not in the listed order, though!

**TRIASSIC**
**CRETACEOUS**
**JURASSIC**

**JAWS**
**EXTINCT**
**FOSSIL**
**CLAW**

**REPTILE**
**PREDATOR**
**HERBIVORE**
**CARNIVORE**

**SCAVENGER**
**PREHISTORIC**

START →

| J | U | R | A | S | E | T | A | C | E |
|---|---|---|---|---|---|---|---|---|---|
| R | P | C | I | S | R | H | S | U | O |
| E | E | P | L | E | C | E | T | O | R |
| D | R | T | I | I | B | R | S | C | I |
| A | S | W | A | V | E | H | I | T | R |
| T | O | R | J | O | R | S | S | A | I |
| A | L | C | E | R | P | I | O | S | S |
| W | E | N | G | E | R | C | F | L | I |
| S | V | N | I | V | O | R | E | E | X |
| C | A | R | A | C | T | C | N | I | T |

# ANIMAL ANTICS

Can you spot six things that are wrong in this picture?

# CASTAWAY

Imagine you've been cast away on a desert island. Draw the things you would most like to have with you.

# SHOE SUMS

Work out the answers to the sums using the number code.
What do all the answers have in common?

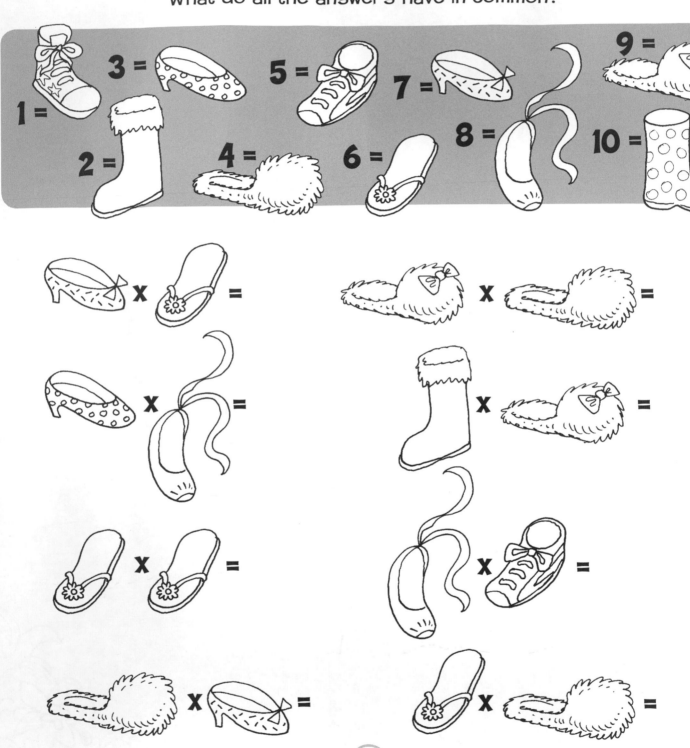

# GROW YOUR OWN

If you could design your own new plant, what would it look like?
Would it have flowers, or spikes, or bug-traps?

## NAME YOUR NEW DISCOVERY

- - - - - - - - - - - - - - - - - -

# MIND THE MINOTAUR

Can you find your way through the maze to escape
the clutches of the angry minotaur?

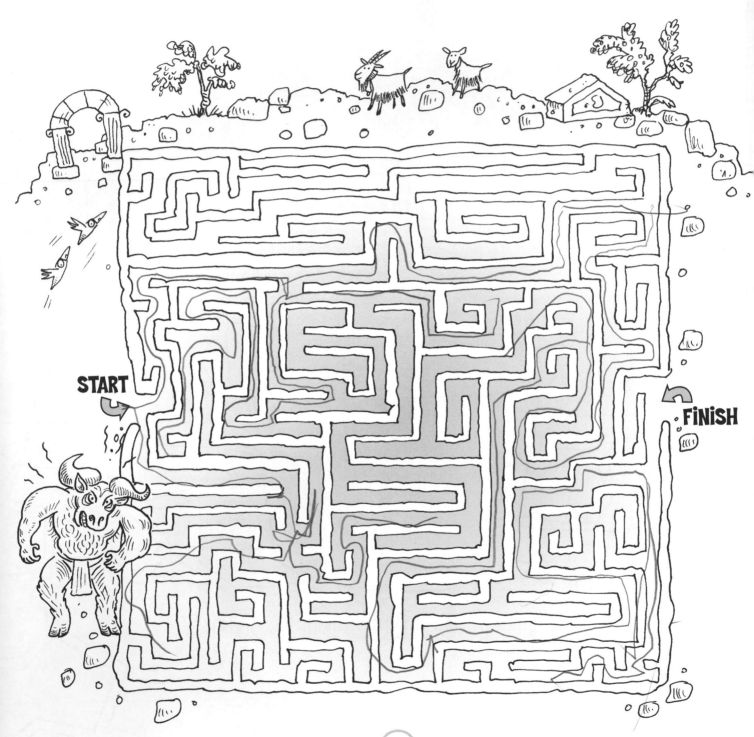

START

FINISH

# EGGS-ACTLY

Fill this nest with dinosaur eggs and babies hatching out of them.

# WHOSE HORSE?

Use the clues to find out which horse belongs to each rider.

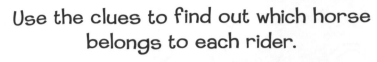

**1.** Ben's horse is called Niko. It isn't palamino.
**2.** Charlie's horse isn't black or called Gunner.
**3.** The horse called Dario is chestnut.

|  | Chestnut | Palamino | Black | Niko | Gunner | Dario |
|---|---|---|---|---|---|---|
| Joe |  |  |  |  |  |  |
| Charlie |  |  |  |  |  |  |
| Ben |  |  |  |  |  |  |

# A MESS OF MUSKETS

How many muskets are there in this pile?

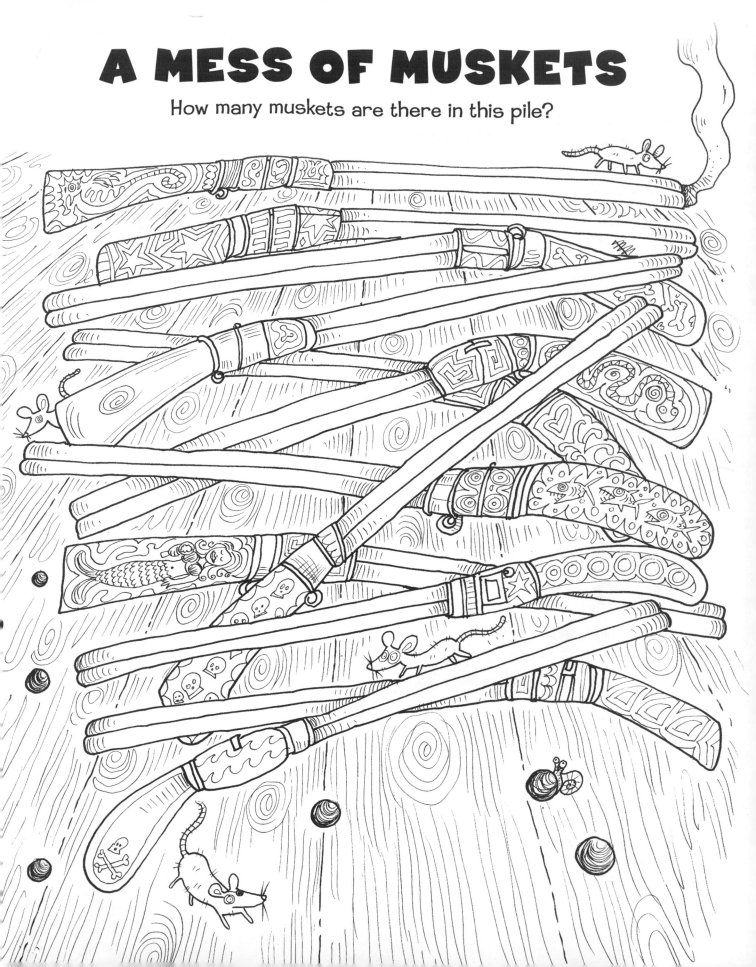

# HIDE AND SEEK

The mini-grid appears once in the whole of the larger grid. Can you find it?

# HOME SWEET HOME

In each row, cross out any letter that appears twice.
The remaining letters spell animal homes - can you
match them to the correct creatures?

P P S C T A T W V O O E S W

Y A Y H C i C V T T E A L L

M O O W U E B U K K M

C F F H P O P L U U T R R C

H A L A O T T D i i G V E V H

Y N X X E S L T L B B Y M M

# TOXIC TERROR

Which of the small pictures matches the main picture of the Toxic Terror?

# GOING, GOING, GONE

Can you find the word EXTINCT hidden just once in this grid? Look up, down, across and diagonally.

| E | X | E | T | i | N | C | T | E | C |
|---|---|---|---|---|---|---|---|---|---|
| X | i | N | C | T | E | X | C | i | T |
| T | T | X | E | X | i | T | E | X | T |
| E | X | T | T | X | E | T | X | E | T |
| T | X | i | N | C | T | E | T | X | X |
| E | X | T | C | E | T | i | i | i | T |
| X | E | T | i | X | E | X | C | T | E |
| C | X | i | N | N | X | N | i | T | X |
| i | i | T | C | N | C | C | T | X | E |
| T | T | C | T | T | C | T | E | X | T |

# MIAOW MIX

Make up a crazy pet that is a mixture of a cat,
a dog and a mouse.

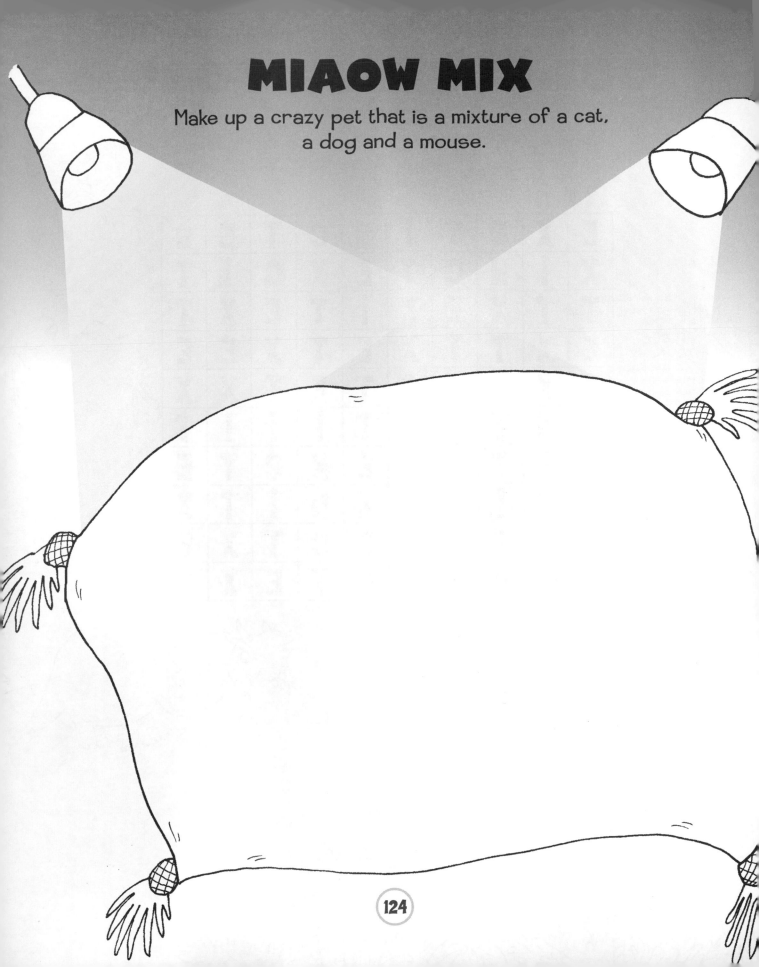

# CODE CRACKER

Solve the sums and cross out each answer in the grid. You should have four remaining numbers to unlock the code on the treasure chest.

50 x 50 =

1800 ÷ 9 =

1234 + 1234 =

6 x 70 =

3000 – 123 =

12 x 12 =

1998 ÷ 2 =

1000 – 55 =

9876 – 22 =

11 x 11 =

8 x 800 =

5555 + 4321 =

448 ÷ 2 =

100 – 36 =

| 2 | 8 | 7 | 7 | 3 | 9 | 9 | 9 |
|---|---|---|---|---|---|---|---|
| 4 | 2 | 0 | 2 | 0 | 0 | 6 | 8 |
| 4 | 2 | 9 | 4 | 5 | 9 | 4 | 7 |
| 1 | 2 | 1 | 6 | 5 | 0 | 0 | 6 |
| 6 | 4 | 9 | 8 | 5 | 4 | 0 | 7 |

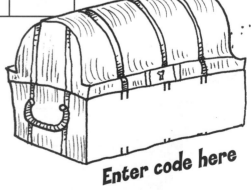

Enter code here

# SHOPPING TRIP

Work out how much it will cost to buy all of the goodies in the circle.

**2.00**

**1.50**

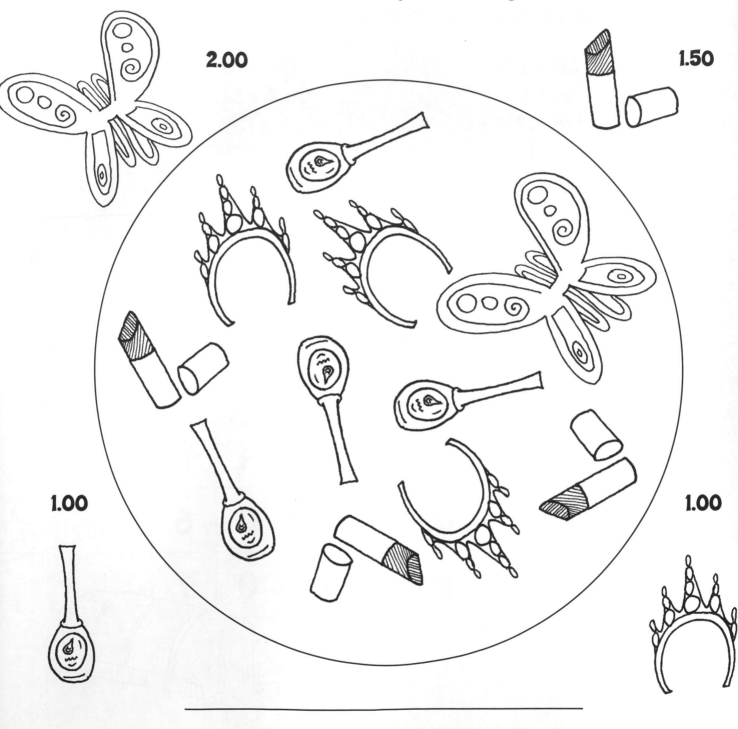

**1.00**

**1.00**

# MEMORY TEST

Study this scene and then turn the page to see how many questions you can answer from memory.

# MEMORY TEST

## Questions:

What is in the big hollow tree?

_____

How many girls are in the picture?

_____

Is there a stag beetle in the picture?

_____

How many birds are flying under the rope bridge?

_____

What four-footed creature is in one of the trees?

_____

# TWO BY TWO

Circle the letters under the two-legged dinosaurs
to spell the name of a dinosaur hunter.

P    i    N    A    L

E    O    N    D    T

i    O    A    L    O

G    i    S    E    T

# HMMMM, TRICKY

Which of these hummingbirds does not have an identical twin?

# WHICH WAY NOW?

Answer the sums correctly to work your way through the compasses from start to finish.

START

8-4

8

6 → 4+4

11

10 → 3+9

12 → 8-1

4

3

9

7

10 ← 5+7 12 → 9+3 14 → 6+1 7 → 9-3 6 →

11

12

8

12

6 ← 6+4 4 → 7-2 5 → 5+4 1 → 8+4 8 →

13

9

9

12

7

4+3

5

9-5

5

8+6

12

6+2

8

12 →

14 →

6 →

15 ← 3+7 10 → 6+5 13 → 11-7 4 → 5-3 2 →

11

3

2

FINISH

# HAPPY HENNA

Add some more henna designs to these beautiful hands.

# SPELLING BEE

Which of these words are correct? And can you correct the other spellings on the spare lines?

potatos ✔ ✗

wolf ✔ ✗

puppys ✔ ✗

telescope ✔ ✗

fungus ✔ ✗

beatiful ✔ ✗

meateorite ✔ ✗

garden ✔ ✗

fierce ✔ ✗

cobbweb ✔ ✗

volcanoe ✔ ✗

_____          _____

_____          _____

_____          _____

# CREEPY CASTLE

Add windows, doors and lots of creepy ghosts and ghouls
to turn this into the most haunted building in the town.

# COME FLY WITH ME

Each of these flying reptiles has a matching twin - except one. Can you spot the odd one out?

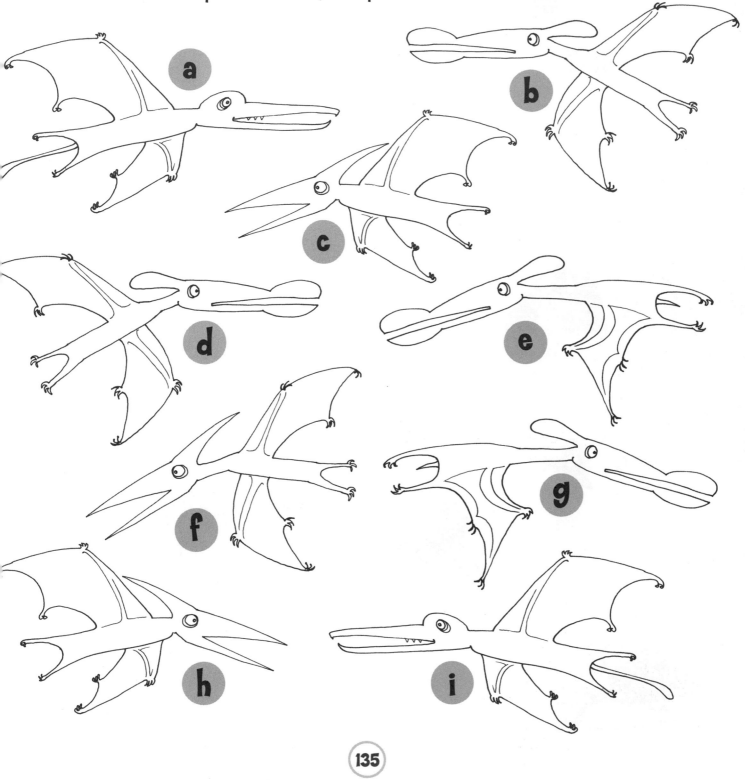

# BIG IS BEST

Which killer whale has the sum which is the biggest number?

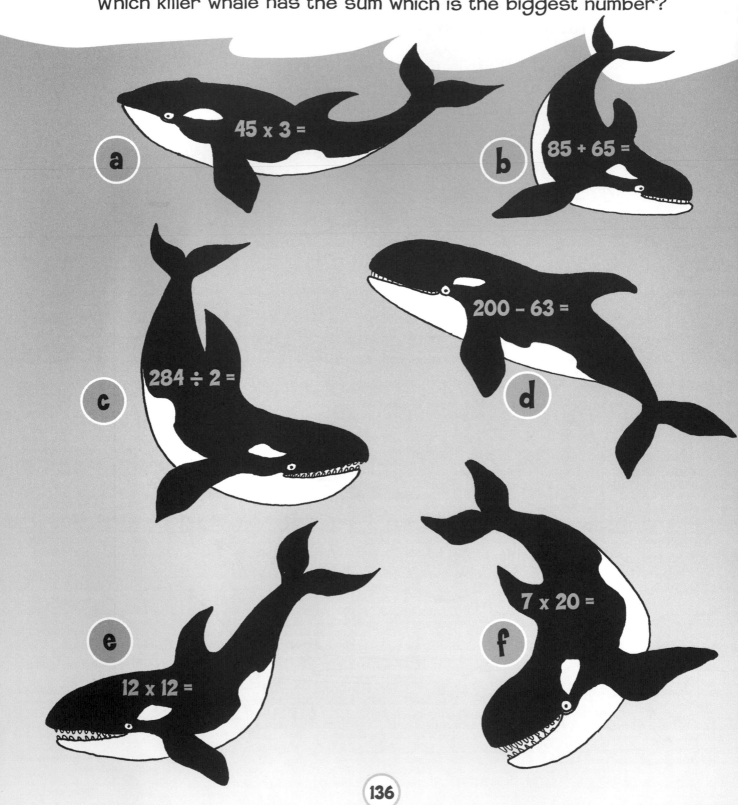

a) $45 \times 3 =$

b) $85 + 65 =$

c) $284 \div 2 =$

d) $200 - 63 =$

e) $12 \times 12 =$

f) $7 \times 20 =$

# FLYING THE FLAG

Design your own pirate flag using the examples
around the edge to give you some ideas.

# SHADY LADY

Which of the silhouettes matches the picture of the ballerina?

# GOTCHA!

This bug is having his lunch... but who is about to gobble him up?

# GONE APE

King Kong has gone crazy and ripped up all these sums. Can you match the equations into pairs, like the example?

3 x 4

5 x 2 = 30 ÷ 3

12½ + 12½

0.5 x 100

2 x 6

5 x 5

35 ÷ 5

50 - 14

25 x 2

6 x 6

½ x 14

# DINO PARK

Draw a map for your very own dinosaur theme park.

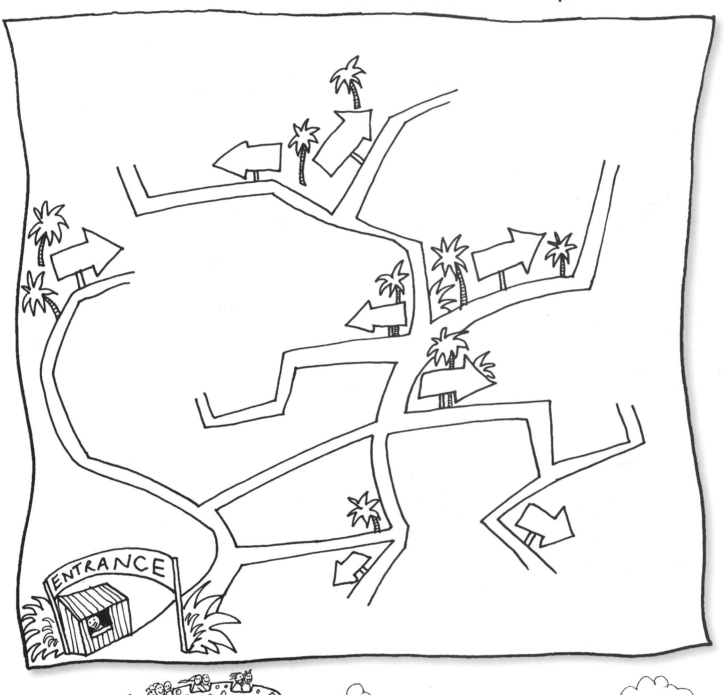

# I SEE!

Cross out the words using the instructions below.
The words left will be the answer to the joke.

**What has six eyes but can't see?**

1. Any word containing the letter **A**.
2. Anything ending with **T**.
3. Words beginning with **L**.

| AN | BAD | GLASSES | ANGRY |
|------|------|---------|-------|
| THREE | LION | ANIMALS | MIGHT |
| CATCH | SENT | LOOK | APES |
| LIGHT | WENT | BLIND | PUT |
| MICE | OUT | FIGHT | LOST |

# ISLAND HOPPING

Use the three-letter words to fill in the gaps
and make the names of six islands.

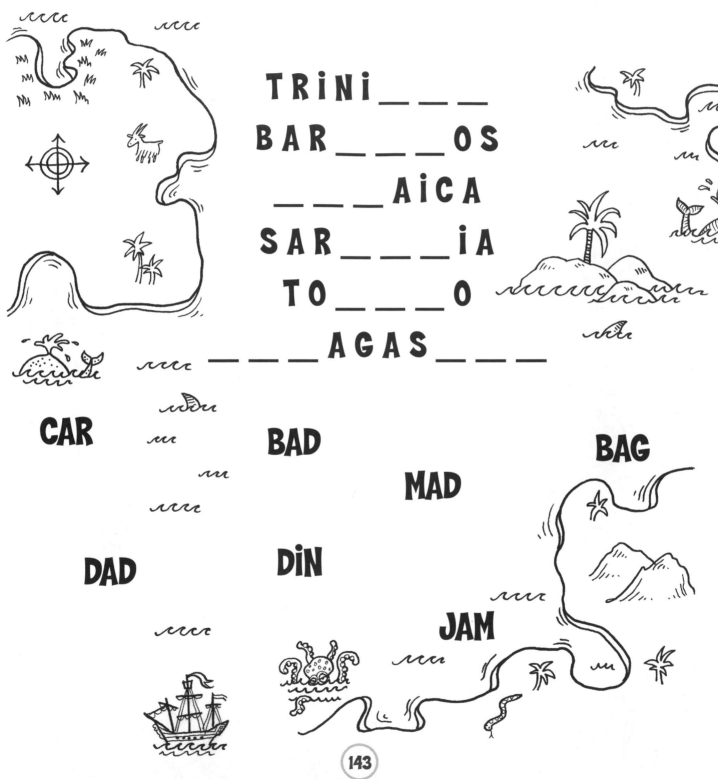

TRINI _ _ _

BAR _ _ _ OS

_ _ _ AICA

SAR _ _ _ IA

TO _ _ _ O

_ _ _ AGAS _ _ _

CAR

BAD

MAD

BAG

DAD

DIN

JAM

# IN THE MIDDLE

Fill in the missing letters to complete the 7-letter words
and spell the name of Princess Leonie's dream pet.

R E Q _ E S T
A B A _ D O N
A C H _ E V E
B U T _ H E R
T H R _ U G H
W A R _ i O R
P A i _ T E R

# IN THEIR PRIME

There are 25 prime numbers below 100 - can you colour every cell that contains a prime number?

3  13  23  6  11  68  9  79  22

7  66  63  99  17  18  24

25  16  5  15  35  45  67  72

88  26  19  27  61  14  33

19  12  89  90  93  97  74  73  71

55  57  77  4  2  28

83  75  81  82  37  38  40  41

52  8  87  91  94  96  53

56  92  47  29  46  49  43  51

59  63  70  20  99  31  21  10

# LOOK OUT!

Take a careful look at the picture to see if you can spot all of the items from the list.

**Find these items!**

# VERY FUNNY

Shade in all the squares containing the letters F, M and R. The letters you have left will spell out the answer to the joke.

**Why do Velociraptors eat raw meat?**

| F | R | M | F | R | M | F | M | M | F | R | F |
| F | B | R | E | F | R | M | M | F | R | M | R |
| M | F | F | M | R | C | F | A | R | F | R | U |
| R | R | M | F | M | R | S | F | E | M | F | U |
| M | M | R | R | F | M | R | R | F | R | M | R |
| T | F | M | H | M | F | E | M | R | Y | R | F |
| R | M | F | R | F | R | M | F | F | M | F | M |
| F | D | M | M | O | M | R | N | F | R | T | R |
| M | R | K | F | R | N | F | F | O | R | M | W |
| H | M | F | R | O | F | M | W | M | F | M | R |
| M | F | R | F | M | R | F | R | M | T | O | F |
| F | C | F | M | O | M | O | F | K | R | F | R |

_____

# SPOTS AND STRIPES

Add patterns to these animals - but use your
imagination. Try zebra stripes on a leopard!

# ID PARADE

Study the sequence of pictures correctly and work out which pirate finishes the pattern: a, b or c?

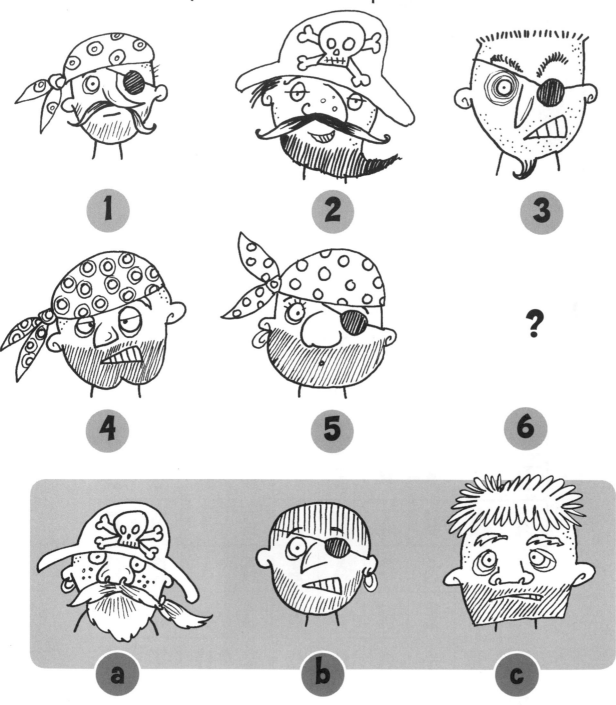

# HIDDEN GEMS

Find each of the gems hidden in the wordsearch grid.

| TURQUOISE | RUBY |
|---|---|
| AMETHYST | JADE |
| AQUAMARINE | SAPPHIRE |
| DIAMOND | OPAL |
| EMERALD | TOPAZ |
| PEARL | MOONSTONE |

| E | Z | A | P | T | P | E | A | R | L |
|---|---|---|---|---|---|---|---|---|---|
| R | D | i | A | S | E | M | A | D | J |
| i | U | G | R | Y | L | E | M | i | O |
| H | S | B | P | H | T | A | E | A | J |
| P | G | A | Y | T | O | Q | P | M | A |
| P | S | A | P | E | P | U | H | O | D |
| A | Q | U | A | M | A | R | i | N | E |
| S | U | A | G | A | Z | A | i | D | U |
| R | A | E | M | E | R | A | L | D | O |
| E | S | i | O | U | Q | R | U | T | P |
| B | M | O | O | N | S | T | O | N | E |

# FOOTPRINTS

Find the correct path from start to finish, following the footprints in this order in any direction:

1)   2)   3)

**START**

**FINISH**

# WITCH'S BREW

If A=1, B=2, C=3 and so on, can you work out what ingredients are being used to make the witch's potions?

19.20.9.14.11
23.15.18.20

23.15.12.6
6.1.14.7

2.1.20
2.18.5.1.20.8

4.18.1.7.15.14
8.5.1.18.20.19

3.18.15.23.19
6.5.5.20

19.14.1.9.12
19.12.9.13.5

# USE YOUR HEAD

How many smaller words can you make from the this dinosaur's name?

## PACHYCEPHALOSAURUS

1    HAPPY

2    LOSER

3

4

5

6

7

8

9

10

11

12

# PENGUIN PARADE

Find the small squares in the main picture and write the grid reference for each one. The first one has been done for you.

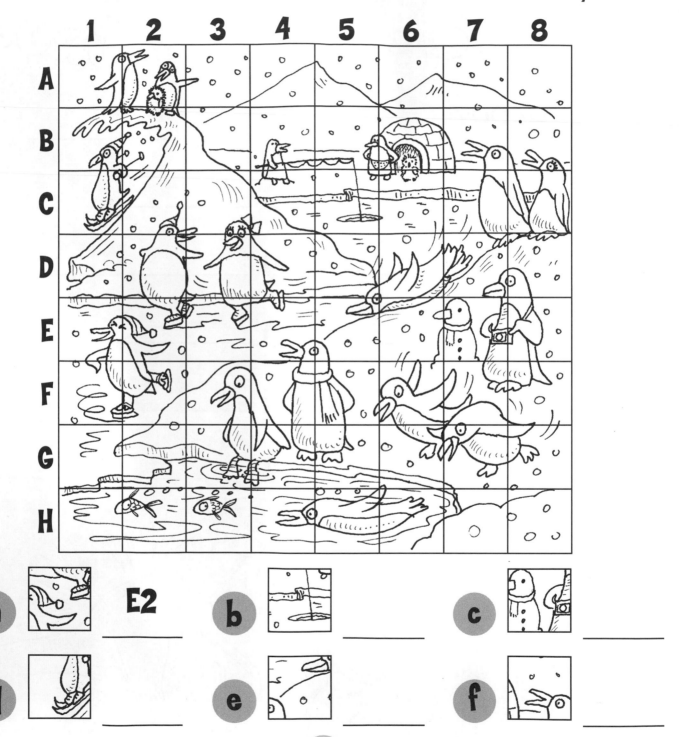

a   **E2**

b   _____

c   _____

d   _____

e   _____

f   _____

# FOLLOW THE TRAIL

Which of the peg-legged pirates has found the treasure?

# HAPPY BIRTHDAY

Finish these scrummy cakes with toppings and decorations. Add birthday candles if you like!

# FUNNY BUG

Shade in all the squares containing D, L or M and use the remaining letters to find the answer to the joke.

What is green and can jump a mile in a minute?

| D | A | L | L | M | L | D | M | M | D |
|---|---|---|---|---|---|---|---|---|---|
| L | D | G | M | R | A | D | L | L | L |
| D | M | L | M | D | M | S | S | L | D |
| L | D | H | O | M | D | L | M | L | D |
| M | M | D | L | P | P | D | D | M | L |
| D | L | L | M | L | D | M | E | R | M |
| W | D | L | D | i | D | L | T | M | H |
| L | M | L | L | D | L | D | M | M | L |
| D | H | M | i | L | L | M | C | C | D |
| M | D | U | L | L | P | D | L | S | M |

_____

# MAKE A MONSTER

This monster is nowhere near scary enough! What will you add to make it more scream-some?

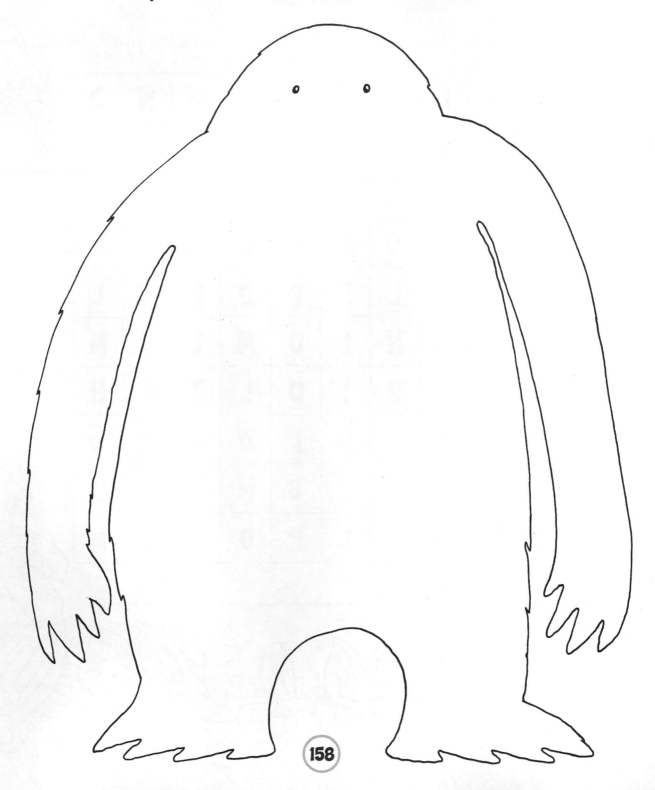

# FOSSIL FRIEND

Cross out every other letter, starting with L, to find a
flying creature from the age of the dinosaurs.

~~L~~ A ~~L~~ B R ~~i~~ C ~~N~~ H T ~~A~~ C ~~E~~ M

O ~~i~~ P ~~N~~ T ~~V~~ E ~~W~~ R ~~S~~ Y ~~U~~ X

The creature is: _ _ _ _ _ _ _ _ _ _ _ _ _

159

# COOL FOR CATS

Find the names of these beautiful creatures hidden in the grid.

BOBCAT    JAGUAR    OCELOT
CARACAL    LEOPARD    SERVAL
CHEETAH    LION    TIGER
COUGAR    LYNX    WILDCAT

| L | J | A | G | C | A | R | A | C | A | L | L | L |
| N | O | C | E | L | O | T | Y | H | W | E | C | C |
| X | H | L | V | A | I | X | T | L | I | O | N | N |
| T | C | I | O | G | C | L | I | G | L | P | X | X |
| B | H | O | E | L | H | J | S | V | A | A | T | T |
| O | E | R | U | S | A | E | E | T | B | R | L | L |
| B | E | Y | T | G | E | L | R | X | O | D | E | E |
| C | H | E | E | T | A | H | V | L | B | C | O | O |
| A | J | L | S | E | L | R | A | U | G | A | J | J |
| T | Y | A | E | Y | E | E | L | O | T | Y | B | B |
| C | V | A | N | W | I | L | D | C | A | T | O | O |
| H | T | X | J | A | G | X | B | O | B | C | B | B |

# WALK THE PLANK!

Can you spot six differences between these two pirate scenes?

# ONCE UPON A TIME

How many smaller words can you make from the letters below?

## FAIRY GODMOTHER

1 _____ FAIR

2 _____ MOTH

3 _____

4 _____

5 _____

6 _____

7 _____

8 _____

9 _____

10 _____

11 _____

12 _____

# WHATEVER THE WEATHER

Look out of this window and draw the kind of weather you like best - is it snowy or sunny, windy or wet?

# LOSING YOUR HEAD

Work out which of the heads originally belonged to the poor headless horseman!

**1.** He had a moustache but no beard.
**2.** He had straight hair.
**3.** He did not wear a bowtie.

a

b

c

d

e

# DINOSAUR MASH-UP

What would a Stegosaurus look like if it got mixed up with a Triceratops?

# RACCOON PONTOON

Find two raccoons on this page that have numbers that add up to 21.

# CANNONBALL RUN

Add up the numbers on each cannonball trail to see which one has been shot the farthest.

# WHO GOES THERE?

Who is coming to visit Princess Naomi?
Tilt the page toward you to read the answer.

PRINCE CHARMING

# A RARE FIND

Some orchids are extremely rare. Can you find the
word ORCHID hidden just once in the grid?

| O | R | C | C | O | R | H | I | D | O |
|---|---|---|---|---|---|---|---|---|---|
| R | C | H | I | R | O | R | O | R | R |
| C | O | D | I | H | R | O | R | C | H |
| D | R | O | D | I | O | C | C | O | H |
| I | C | O | O | D | I | H | C | R | D |
| D | R | O | R | R | O | I | O | O | D |
| O | R | R | D | O | C | D | D | I | O |
| H | I | C | O | C | O | C | H | D | R |
| D | C | H | R | H | I | D | H | C | D |
| O | R | I | D | R | I | C | O | R | H |
| R | H | D | H | I | D | O | R | O | C |
| O | R | C | H | D | D | O | O | O | R |

# CRACKING UP

Can you join up the broken pieces to make the
names of eight scary creatures?

DRA

SPI

ZOM

MED

GOR

GOB

KRA

SPH

KEN

iNX

DER

LiN

USA

GON

GON

BiE

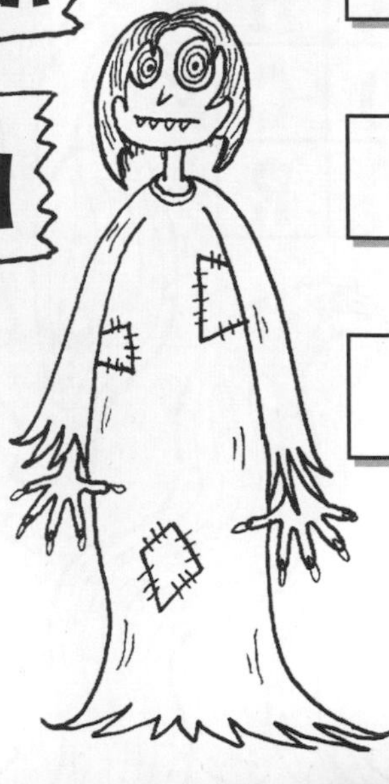

# ON DISPLAY

Help the museum curator unscramble the letters to put a proper sign by her dinosaur display.

| D | O | O | R | N | O | T |
|---|---|---|---|---|---|---|

|  |  |  |  |  |  |  |
|---|---|---|---|---|---|---|

# IN THE JUNGLE

Zoologists find new creatures in the deepest jungle. What is hiding here?

# TAKE A LOOK

Take a careful look at the picture to see if you can spot all of the items from the list below.

**Find these items!**

# GRIDLOCKED

Shade in all the squares containing O, M or B and use the remaining letters to spell out a classic fairy tale.

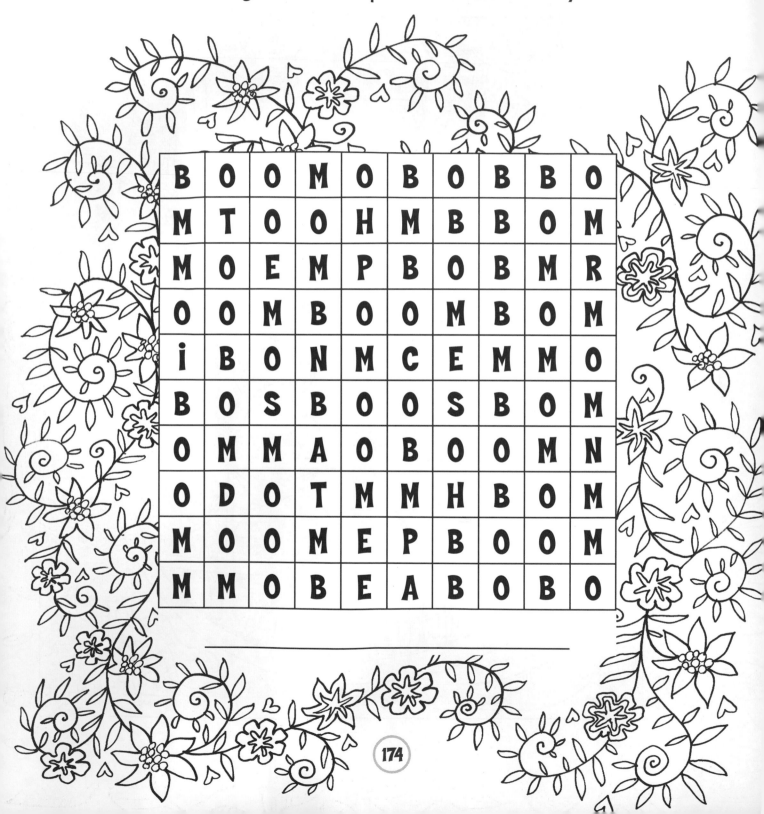

_____

# I SPIED A SPIDER

How many camouflaged spiders can you spy in this leafy pile? Once you've counted them, finish the picture.

# DUMMY MUMMY

This mummy isn't very clever. Can you help it find the correct scarab beetle to open the Book of the Dead?

77

144 ÷ 2

12 X 7

43 + 34

12 + 55

4 X 9

100 - 33

# MIND THE GAPS

Use the three-letter words from the list to fill the gaps and complete the dinosaur names.

**ALL    CAN    HER    PAT    RAP**
**BAR    DIP    NOT    PIN    TIN**

GIGA __ __ __ OSAURUS

__ __ __ YONYX

VELOCI __ __ __ TOR

ACRO __ __ __ THOSAURUS

__ __ __ OSAURUS

S __ __ __ OSAURUS

__ __ __ RERASAURUS

ARGEN __ __ __ OSAURUS

__ __ __ PLODOCUS

A __ __ __ TOSAURUS

# PETS WIN PRIZES

Draw some stunning pets winning Best in Class!

# ALL AT SEA

Help the pirate row to the safety of the island
by finding a way through the maze.

# WHERE OH WHERE?

Crack the code to find out where Princess Dulcibella is dreaming she might go.

# FANGS A LOT

Which of the numbers on Dracula's cape are
NOT in the nine times table?

18
54 63 72
81 27 89

52
66 36 45
31 47 99

# MAP IT OUT

Draw your own map to remind you where to find your buried treasure.

# Answers

## 3 GOING APE

Find these items!

## 4 MISSING MONSTER

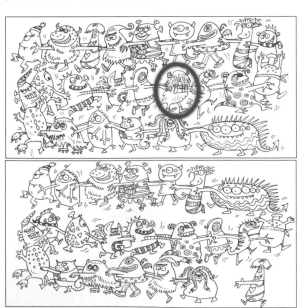

## 5 PIRATE PAIRS

## 7 ALL MIXED UP

CACTUS
WILLOW
ORCHID
BONSAI
FUNGUS
NETTLE
BAMBOO
CROCUS
CLOVER
VIOLET

## 9 JURASSIC JOKE

Tyrannosaurus wrecks!

## 10 EGGS-ACTLY

Toucan

## 11 WEIRD SEARCH

| Z | L | V | A | M | P | I | R | E | G |
|---|---|---|---|---|---|---|---|---|---|
| W | L | W | I | Z | L | G | F | G | Z |
| O | I | O | A | G | L | L | H | N | O |
| E | E | Z | G | H | O | O | D | A | M |
| W | W | Z | A | W | R | W | G | I | B |
| O | G | W | E | R | T | I | W | T | I |
| L | G | R | I | E | D | Z | E | R | E |
| L | E | R | Y | T | E | V | R | A | R |
| W | E | E | F | W | C | A | E | M | A |
| W | G | H | T | S | O | H | G | E | W |

## 12 POLLEN COUNT

a 29
b 13
c 12
d 97

## 14 OUT OF THIS WORLD!

b

## 16 SEEING STRIPES

d

## 17 THE NAME GAME

Gonzalo

## 18 BUTWTERFLY BONANZA

h

## 21 TRICERATOPS TRAIL

## 23 IN A MUDDLE

Bermuda

## 25 BIG IS BEAUTIFUL

7 x 3 x 2 = 42

## 27 MUNCH TIME

e

## 28 THE RIGHT FIT

The circled letters spell hedgehog.

| H | O | R | N | B | I | L | L |
|---|---|---|---|---|---|---|---|
| E | L | E | P | H | A | N | T |
| A | A | R | D | V | A | R | K |
| F | L | A | M | I | N | G | O |
| P | A | R | A | K | E | E | T |
| C | H | I | P | M | U | N | K |
| M | O | N | G | O | O | S | E |
| B | U | L | L | F | R | O | G |

## 30 FAIRY FOOD

a

## 31 HONEY TRAP

2 bees are going back to the hive.

## 32 ON REFLECTION

What do vampire movie stars often receive?
Fang mail!

## 34 FEEDING TIME

Deer, lion, puma, seal, wolf, boar

## 35 MANY MAGGOTS

$40 + 63 = 103$
$72 - 53 = 19$
$81 \div 9 = 9$
$5 \times 6 = 30$
$27 + 27 = 54$
$86 - 39 = 47$
$7 \times 3 = 21$
$48 \div 6 = 8$

## 36 IVORY TOWER

b

**37  A BIRD'S EYE VIEW**

e

**39  DINO DIGITS**

a = h
b = e
c = g
d = f

**40  MONSTER MATCH**

b and f

**41  LAND AHOY!**

**42  DANDELION CLOCK**

Lunchtime

## 43 A-MAZING

## 45 DINOSAURS AND DRAGONS

## 46 PAIR UP THE PETS

Annika has a brown dog.
Luke has a black cat.
Freddie has a white hamster.

## 48 SHOE SHUFFLE

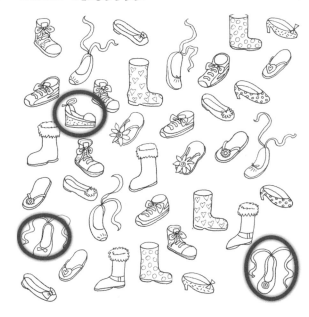

## 49 GOING UNDERGROUND

Mole, groundhog, badger

## 50 SPELL SHOP

2 x bat's wings = 1 gold coin
4 x cat's eyes = 4 gold coins
1.5 m spider web = 3 gold coins
1 jar of nightfall = 7 gold coins

Total = 15 gold coins

## 52 THINK ABOUT IT

A polygon!

## 53 MINI BEASTS

A beetle (each row and column has one of each creature)

## 55 PRETTY POLLY

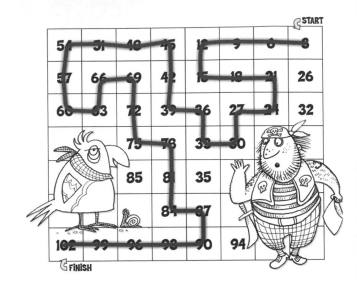

## 56 FORTUNE TELLING

Banshee, werewolf

## 57 TOO TROO

9

## 54 CAGE CODE

6924

## 59 SEADOG SUDOKU

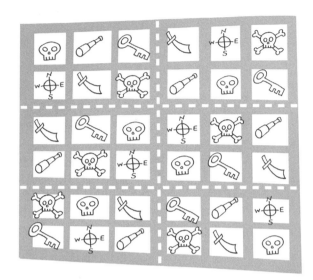

## 60 RING RING

Ring a (each column has one of each design, each row has the same design at both ends)

## 62 BEASTLY BEING

GOGLEYOR

## 63 DINOSAUR WORLD

1. D1
2. E3
3. Ice cream
4. T. rex

## 65 BARREL OF FUN

| A | A | Y | Y | H | A | O | A | Y | H | O | Y |
| A | H | A | O | A | A | H | H | O | O | H | A |
| O | H | A | O | H | A | O | A | Y | A | Y |
| A | H | Y | H | O | H | O | H | O | O | Y | O |
| A | H | A | O | O | Y | Y | O | Y | H | H |
| H | Y | E | Y | A | O | Y | H | H | A | H |
| Y | A | O | A | H | Y | Y | A | Y | O | O | O |
| A | H | Y | H | A | H | O | Y | A | O | H | A |
| Y | O | O | H | A | H | A | H | O | A | Y | H |
| A | H | A | A | H | O | Y | A | O | O | H | A |
| H | O | Y | H | O | A | H | O | O | A | O | H |
| O | H | H | Y | H | O | Y | O | H | O | Y | O |
| A | O | H | O | Y | A | H | Y | O | H | A | H |
| A | H | A | H | A | Y | O | H | O | Y | O | O |

## 66 RIGHT ROYAL WRONGS

1. The bird is flying upside down
2. One guest has a sleeping cat on her hat
3. The bride's bouquet is made of fish
4. The groom's crown is on upside down
5. Another guest is wearing a snorkel
6. There is a monkey swinging from the bunting!

## 67 TREE TIMES TABLE

a $7 \times 3 = 21$
b $5 \times 5 = 25$
c $3 \times 4 = 12$
d $5 \times 3 = 15$
e $0 \times 8 = 0$
f $30 \div 3 = 10$
g $9 \times 3 = 27$
h $12 \div 4 = 3$
i $6 \times 6 = 36$
j $2 \div 7 = 3$

## 69 TIME OUT

a Plateosaurus
b Velociraptor

## 70 CREATURE CARVINGS

26 (not including the owl sitting on a branch!)

## 72 WISH ME LUCK

## 73 BEETLE MANIA

d

## 74 MONSTER LAUGHS

Because he wanted a light snack!

## 76 NEW FACES

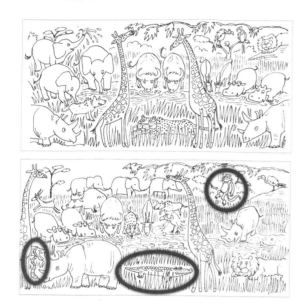

## 79 NATURE HUNT

| W | A | R | U | T | W | I | L | L | O | W |
|---|---|---|---|---|---|---|---|---|---|---|
| S | B | E | E | C | H | U | E | T | L | G |
| Y | O | R | S | B | B | A | Q | E | N | R |
| C | A | X | P | F | Q | M | P | H | V | P |
| A | V | R | C | N | J | T | I | S | Z | O |
| M | K | G | A | W | C | L | W | O | F | O |
| O | A | K | T | B | C | H | M | I | T | P |
| R | S | Y | L | R | X | K | C | Y | G | L |
| E | M | R | D | Y | U | F | D | L | K | A |
| Z | C | H | E | S | T | N | U | T | N | R |
| G | L | E | K | P | N | G | K | E | X | M |
| B | A | S | H | R | Z | I | W | H | U | F |
| J | H | A | F | O | O | P | I | N | E | L |
| E | U | D | B | C | I | S | C | J | D | Q |
| A | P | P | L | E | T | P | C | V | K | E |

## 77 PIRATE LOGIC

Ship 1 is owned by Captain Barnacle who has a big parrot called Perky.

Ship 2 is owned by Captain Greybeard who has a small parrot called Pesky.

Ship 3 is owned by Captain Scablegs who has a medium sized parrot called Potty.

## 80  CHAIN REACTION

Piece d

## 81  FOSSIL FINDER

Deinonychus, Ankylosaurus, Diplodocus, Iguanodon, Spinosaurus, Oviraptor

## 82  MONKEY PUZZLE

Elephant, hippopotamus, rhinoceros

## 83  FINDING YOUR WAY

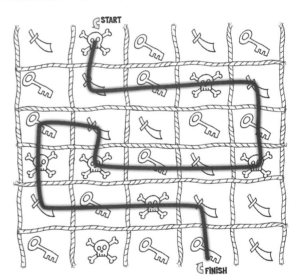

## 84  TOWER TABLES

44

## 86 MEET THE MISFITS

Female a (follow the patterns: the ladies have alternate long sleeves and short sleeves, alternate short hair and long hair, and alternate ragged hem or straight hem)

## 87 DINO DAZE

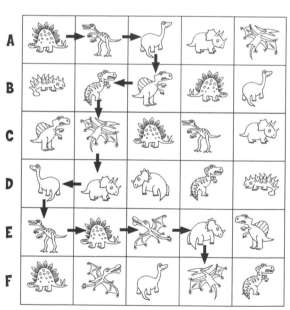

## 89 SAFE PORT

The pirates should land in C5.

## 90 CROWNING GLORY

Peru

## 91 THROUGH THE LOOKING GLASS

e

## 93 DINO-DOKU

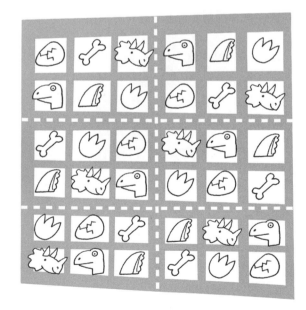

## 94 CAT CONUNDRUM

THERMAP doesn't unscramble to spell a big cat.
The others can be rearranged to spell jaguar, tiger, cheetah, leopard, ocelot and cougar.

## 96 MIRROR MIRROR

The snow ball!

## 97 AS THE CROW FLIES

Crow a flew the farthest:
a 16 + 53 + 41 + 8 = 118
b 29 + 37 + 18 + 21 = 105
c 48 + 13 + 31 + 17 = 109
d 14 + 62 + 21 + 18 = 115

## 98 SPOOKY SPELLINGS

Here are some you might have thought of:
NUT, WET, GNU,
HIGH, WRITE, TWIG,
UNIT, HURT, TWIN,
WING, GRUNT, TRUTH,
NIGHT, THOUGH, THROUGH

## 100 REALLY RARE

| P | A | N | N | A | P | N | A |
|---|---|---|---|---|---|---|---|
| N | P | D | N | A | A | A | P |
| D | A | N | P | D | N | D | A |
| A | D | A | A | P | D | N | N |
| P | A | P | A | N | D | A | A |
| P | A | N | N | A | D | N | P |
| A | A | D | D | P | D | A | N |
| A | N | D | A | A | D | D | N |
| A | P | A | D | D | P | A | N |
| N | A | D | A | N | A | D | P |
| D | N | A | P | A | N | N | A |
| A | A | P | N | N | D | A | D |
| D | P | A | D | N | D | D | N |
| N | A | N | N | P | A | N | A |
| A | N | D | P | A | D | N | A |

## 101 RUFUS REDBEARD

g

## 102 PRINCESS SUDOKU

## 103 UGLY BUG BALL

## 104 WHO GOES THERE?

Godzilla

## 105 THUMBS UP

These five are correct:
Velociraptor, Gigantosaurus,
Pteranodon, Tyrannosaurus,
Spinosaurus

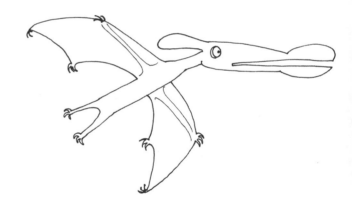

## 106 EAGLE EYES

a belongs to 4
b belongs to 2
c belongs to 1
d belongs to 3

**107  DEADLY DICE**

1 + 4 x 5 is the highest:
6 + 2 x 3 = 24
4 + 3 x 3 = 21
3 + 3 x 4 = 24
1 + 4 x 5 = 25
2 + 5 x 2 = 14
5 + 6 x 2 = 22

**109  MAKING TRACKS**

Because they look silly in raincoats!

**111  ON THEIR TRAIL**

| J | U | R | A | S | E | T | A | C | E |
|---|---|---|---|---|---|---|---|---|---|
| R | P | C | i | S | R | H | S | U | O |
| E | E | P | L | E | C | E | T | O | R |
| D | R | T | i | B | R | S | C | i |   |
| A | S | W | A | V | E | H | i | T | R |
| T | O | R | J | O | R | S | S | A | R |
| A | L | C | E | R | P | i | O | S | S |
| W | E | N | G | E | R | C | F | L | i |
| S | V | N | i | V | O | R | E | E | X |
| C | A | R | A | C | T | C | N | i | T |

198

## 112 ANIMAL ANTICS

1. The lion has tiger stripes.
2. The giraffe is up to his neck in water.
3. The zebra has a saddle on.
4. A hippo is wearing boots.
5. There is a bouquet of flowers in the reeds.
6. The chimps are playing cards.

## 114 SHOE SUMS

All the answers are even numbers.
7 x 6 = 42
9 x 4 = 36
3 x 8 = 24
2 x 9 = 18
6 x 6 = 36
8 x 5 = 40
4 x 7 = 28
6 x 4 = 24

## 116 MIND THE MINOTAUR

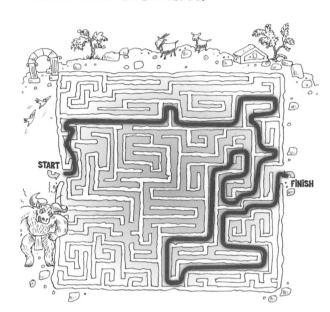

## 118 WHOSE HORSE?

Joe has a palamino horse called Gunner.
Charlie has a chestnut horse called Dario.
Ben has a black horse called Niko.

## 119 A MESS OF MUSKETS

12

## 120 HIDE AND SEEK

## 121 HOME SWEET HOME

Cave = bear
Hive = bee
Web = spider
Hole = fox
Lodge = beaver
Nest = bird

## 122 TOXIC TERROR

d

## 123 GOING, GOING, GONE

| E | X | E | T | i | N | C | T | E | C |
|---|---|---|---|---|---|---|---|---|---|
| X | i | N | C | T | E | X | C | i | T |
| T | T | X | E | i | T | E | X | T | T |
| E | X | T | T | X | E | T | X | E | E |
| T | i | N | C | T | E | T | X | X | X |
| E | X | T | C | E | T | i | i | i | T |
| X | E | T | i | X | E | X | C | T | E |
| C | X | i | N | X | N | i | T | X | X |
| i | i | T | C | N | C | T | X | E | E |
| T | T | C | T | T | C | T | E | X | T |

## 125 CODE CRACKER

50 x 50 = 2500
1800 ÷ 9 = 200
1234 + 1234 = 2468
6 x 70 = 420
3000 - 123 = 2877
12 x 12 = 144
1998 ÷ 2 = 999
1000 - 55 = 945
9876 - 22 = 9854
11 x 11 = 121
8 x 800 = 6400
5555 + 4321 = 9876
448 ÷ 2 = 224
100 - 36 = 64
Code is 3597

## 126 SHOPPING TRIP

2.00 + 4.50 + 4.00 + 3.00 = 13.50

## 128 MEMORY TEST

An owl
2
Yes (on the right-hand tree trunk)
3
Squirrel

## 129 TWO BY TWO

Paleontologist

## 130 HMMMM, TRICKY

## 307 WHICH WAY NOW?

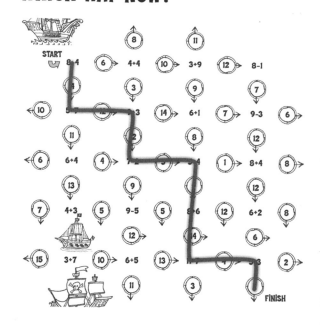

## 309 SPELLING BEE

These words are correct:
wolf, telescope, fungus, garden, fierce
The incorrect ones should be spelt like this:
potatoes, puppies, meteorite, beautiful, cobweb, volcano

(201)

## 135  COME FLY WITH ME

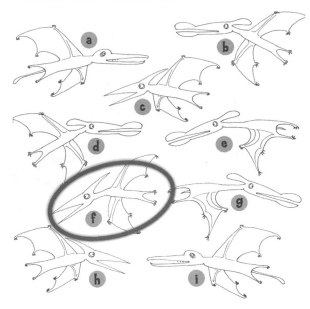

## 136  BIG IS BEST

Sum b because
a = 135
b = 150
c = 142
d = 137
e = 144
f = 140

## 138  SHADY LADY

e

## 140  GONE APE

3 x 4 = 2 x 6
12½ + 12½  = 5 x 5
35 " 5 = ½ x 14
25 x 2 = 0.5 x 100
6 x 6 = 50 - 14

## 142  I SEE!

Three blind mice!

## 143  ISLAND HOPPING

Trinidad, Barbados, Jamaica,
Sardinia, Tobago, Madagascar

## 144  IN THE MIDDLE

The words are:
Request
Abandon
Achieve
Butcher
Through
Warrior
Painter

The word in the middle is
Unicorn

## 145 IN THEIR PRIME

| | | | | | | | | |
|---|---|---|---|---|---|---|---|---|
| 3 | 13 | 23 | 6 | 11 | 68 | 9 | 79 | 22 |
| 7 | 66 | 63 | 99 | 17 | 18 | 24 | | |
| 25 | 16 | | 5 | 15 | 35 | 45 | 67 | 72 |
| 88 | 26 | 19 | | 27 | 61 | 14 | 33 | |
| 19 | 12 | 89 | 90 | 93 | 97 | 74 | 73 | 71 |
| 55 | 57 | 77 | | 4 | 2 | | 28 | |
| 83 | | 75 | 81 | 82 | 37 | 38 | 40 | 41 |
| | 52 | 8 | 87 | 91 | 94 | 96 | 53 | |
| 56 | 92 | 47 | 29 | 46 | 49 | | 43 | 51 |
| 59 | 63 | 70 | 20 | 99 | 31 | 21 | 10 | |

## 147 VERY FUNNY

| F | R | M | F | R | M | F | M | M | F | R | F |
|---|---|---|---|---|---|---|---|---|---|---|---|
| F | B | R | E | F | R | M | M | F | R | M | R |
| M | F | F | M | R | C | F | A | R | F | R | U |
| R | R | R | M | F | M | R | S | F | E | M | F | M |
| M | M | R | R | F | M | R | R | F | R | M | R |
| T | F | M | H | M | F | E | M | R | Y | R | F |
| R | R | M | F | R | F | R | M | F | F | M | F | M |
| F | D | M | M | O | R | N | F | R | T | R |
| M | R | K | F | R | N | F | F | O | R | M | W |
| H | M | F | R | O | F | M | W | M | F | M | R |
| M | F | R | F | M | R | F | R | M | T | O | F |
| F | C | F | M | O | M | O | F | K | R | F | R |

Because they don't know how to cook

## 146 LOOK OUT!

Find these items!

## 149 iD PARADE

Pirate c (The pattern is patch, no patch, patch, no patch... and head gear, head gear, no head gear... so the next pirate must have no patch and nothing on his head).

## 150 HIDDEN GEMS

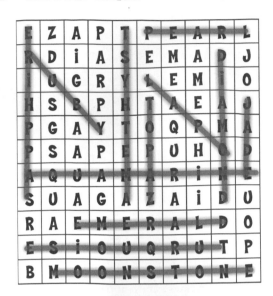

## 151 FOOTPRINTS

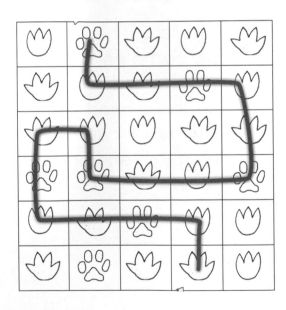

## 152 WITCH'S BREW

Stink wort, wolf fang, crow's feet, bat breath, snail slime, dragon hearts

## 153 USE YOUR HEAD

Here are some you might have thought of:
APE, HOPE, PUSH, HEAP, EASY, HOUR, SOAP, SHOP, HUSH, SHOE, ESSAY, HOUSE, PAUSE, SHAPE, ACCESS

## 154 PENGUIN PARADE

a = E2 b = C5 c = E7
d = C1 e = E5 f = B7

## 155 FOLLOW THE TRAIL

b

## 157 FUNNY BUG

| D | A | L | L | M | L | D | M | M | D |
|---|---|---|---|---|---|---|---|---|---|
| L | D | G | M | R | A | D | L | L | L |
| D | M | L | M | D | M | S | S | L | D |
| L | D | H | O | M | D | L | M | L | D |
| M | M | D | L | P | P | D | D | M | L |
| D | L | L | M | L | D | M | E | R | M |
| W | D | L | D | i | D | L | T | M | H |
| L | M | L | L | D | L | D | M | M | L |
| D | H | M | i | L | L | M | C | C | D |
| M | D | U | L | L | P | D | L | S | M |

A grasshopper with hiccups

## 159 FOSSIL FRIEND

Archaeopteryx

## 160 COOL FOR CATS

| L | J | A | G | C | A | R | A | C | A | L | L |
|---|---|---|---|---|---|---|---|---|---|---|---|
| N | O | C | E | L | O | T | Y | H | W | E | C |
| X | H | L | V | A | i | X | T | L | i | O | N |
| T | C | i | O | G | C | L | i | G | L | P | X |
| B | H | O | E | L | H | J | S | V | A | A | T |
| B | E | R | U | S | A | E | E | T | B | R | L |
| B | E | Y | T | E | L | R | X | O | D | E |   |
| C | H | E | E | T | A | H | V | L | B | C | O |
| A | J | L | S | E | L | R | A | U | G | A | J |
| T | Y | A | E | Y | E | E | L | O | T | Y | B |
| C | V | A | N | W | i | L | D | C | A | T | O |
| H | T | X | J | A | G | X | B | O | B | C | B |

## 161 WALK THE PLANK!

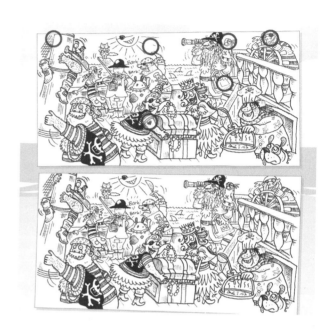

## 162 ONCE UPON A TIME

Here are some you might have thought of:
POT, OUT, ACE, PIN, POEM, INTO, NOON, OPEN, MENU, TEMPO, INPUT, ONION, POUNCE, OPTION, MOTION

## 164 LOSING YOUR HEAD

d

## 166 RACCOON PONTOON

## 167 CANNONBALL RUN

Cannonball a was shot the farthest.
a  30 + 26 + 48 + 25 = 129
b  37 + 14 + 29 + 41 = 121
c  39 + 26 + 27 + 33 = 125

## 168 WHO GOES THERE?

Prince Charming

## 169 A RARE FIND

| O | R | C | C | O | R | H | i | D | O |
| R | C | H | i | R | O | R | O | R | R |
| C | O | D | i | H | R | O | R | C | H |
| D | R | O | D | i | O | C | C | O | H |
| i | C | O | O | D | i | H | C | R | D |
| R | R | O | R | R | O | i | O | O | D |
| O | R | R | O | D | O | C | D | D | O |
| H | i | C | O | C | O | C | H | D | R |
| D | C | H | R | H | i | D | H | C | D |
| O | R | i | D | R | i | C | O | R | H |
| R | H | D | H | i | D | O | R | O | C |
| O | R | C | H | D | D | O | O | O | R |

## 170 CRACKING UP

Dragon, spider, zombie, medusa, gorgon, goblin, kraken, sphinx

## 171 ON DISPLAY

Troodon

## 172 TAKE A LOOK

## 174 GRIDLOCKED

| B | O | O | M | O | B | O | B | B | O |
|---|---|---|---|---|---|---|---|---|---|
| M | T | O | O | H | M | B | B | O | M |
| M | O | E | M | P | B | O | B | M | R |
| O | O | M | B | O | O | M | B | O | M |
| i | B | O | N | M | C | E | M | M | O |
| B | O | S | B | O | O | S | B | O | M |
| O | M | M | A | O | B | O | O | M | N |
| O | D | O | T | M | M | H | B | O | M |
| M | O | O | M | E | P | B | O | O | M |
| M | M | O | B | E | A | B | O | B | O |

The Princess and the Pea

## 175 i SPIED A SPIDER

## 176 DUMMY MUMMY

43 + 34 = 77

## 177 MIND THE GAPS

GigaNOTosaurus,
BARyonyx, VelociRAPtor,
ALLosaurus, sPINosaurus,
ArgenTINosaurus, DIPlodocus,
aPATosaurus

## 178 ALL AT SEA

## 180 WHERE OH WHERE?

Over the rainbow

## 181 FANGS A LOT